THE
RESPONSIBLE
CHRISTIAN

THE
RESPONSIBLE
CHRISTIAN

BY VICTOR OBENHAUS

The University of Chicago Press

Library of Congress Catalog Number: 57-11211

THE UNIVERSITY OF CHICAGO PRESS, CHICAGO 37
Cambridge University Press, London, N.W. 1, England
The University of Toronto Press, Toronto 5, Canada

© 1957 by The University of Chicago. Published 1957
Composed and printed by THE UNIVERSITY OF CHICAGO PRESS
Chicago, Illinois, U.S.A.

To Constance, Helen, and Mark

PREFACE

Strong interest in religion and substantial support of its institutions characterizes present-day life in the United States. Whether this is due to comparative prosperity and a desire not to disturb it or whether it derives from a genuine yearning for stable religious foundations is debatable.

It is a thesis of this book that indifference to society's sore spots breeds irresponsibility and is inimical to the Christian interpretation of life. This indifference sows the wind and reaps the whirlwind. Genuine religious vitality comes from wholehearted engagement with moral and ethical issues. Any pseudoreligiousness achieved apart from these issues is less than wholesome and becomes progressively flabby.

Rich and fervent devotional life is utterly essential to a full-rounded religious experience. When one's devotion ends in one's self, however, it ends. Genuine religious life does not end, for it is eternally characterized by self-expenditure in interests other than one's self.

It is apparent that we have come out of an era of want into an era of abundance, for many people at least. Physical comfort and good feeling have always been mistaken for religiousness and a symbol of divine favor. Whether the human spirit can resist the temptations and atrophy of abundance we do not know. But, despite the era of abundance, there are tough problems in our society requiring solution.

The combination of two factors, then, have prompted my writing this book: the presence of many difficult, unsolved problems and the fact that Christian vitality and faith can be strengthened only by trying to solve them.

The final decision rests with God. However, man as coworker with God in God's created universe is obliged to labor to achieve a better society. All the evidence of religious history indicates that man is summoned to live responsibly in relation to his fellow men.

Obviously, no single individual can be fully informed on all the issues discussed in the following pages. I am of course indebted to innumerable authorities and publishers and I gratefully acknowledge my appreciation to those whose works appear in the footnotes and in the suggested readings.

When I was a student at Oberlin College, a quickening interest in the more inclusive interpretation of the Christian faith was added to the substantial religious foundation supplied to me by my parents and my church. Subsequently, at Union Theological Seminary and at Columbia University, the more profound dimensions of the whole problem became apparent. I owe a considerable debt of gratitude to the former and the present staff of the Council for Social Action of the Congregational-Christian Churches and especially to its director, Ray Gibbons. To the Rev. Cameron P. Hall and the staff and members of the Department of Church and Economic Life of the National Council of Churches, I want to express my very great appreciation both for their personal assistance and for the privilege of using resources for which they are responsible. My colleagues of the Federated Theological Faculty of the University of Chicago have been most generous in counsel and in reducing academic burdens. The Chicago Theological Seminary, the Administrative Council of which I am privileged to be a part, has a rich history of concern for the whole gospel. It has provided aid in ways too numerous to itemize, and without its generosity my task would have been much more difficult. While I was preparing this material, I enjoyed association with Samuel C. Kincheloe, and portions of this volume were discussed in courses we shared. My debt to him is very great. In the early stages of my work on this book, Mrs. Hyral Groves helped with the typing and gave the benefit of her skill in composition. For the preparation of this manuscript, however, I owe more to Mrs. Frances Ritsch than to anyone else. Her patience with many changes and her innumerable helpful suggestions make it a better product than it would otherwise have been.

Finally, no words can satisfactorily express an author's appreciation to his wife for enduring late nights, delayed meals, and curtailed family life and for giving valuable counsel.

Victor Obenhaus

TABLE OF CONTENTS

INTRODUCTION

The message of this book is intended primarily for laymen. Significantly, in each of the major faiths the role of the layman is coming into increasing prominence. Laymen's organizations formed around denominational loyalties or professional and vocational activities are among the most interesting developments of church and synagogue life in our time. Stripped of their labels, the programs and purposes of these organizations related to religious institutions look very much alike. For the same reason that Catholics and Protestants can unite in support of certain major social aims, these laymen's groups find much in common.

Our concern in this volume, however, is not primarily to discover the areas of agreement between the major faiths, important though this be. Rather it is to confront Christians in general and Protestants in particular with the inseparable relation between their faith and the major social issues in American life. This has always been an inherent part of the church's task, emphasized with varying degrees of intensity. Through the manner in which this function of the church and the Christian faith is dealt with in the ensuing pages it is hoped that the church's work may be aided.

Because, in Protestantism at least, the church is people —people devoted to God as we know him in Jesus Christ —it must be through the laymen that the church's work is done. The manner in which laymen bring their faith to bear upon society's most critical issues will test the vitality and depth of their faith. Vitality and depth go together.

On all sides it becomes apparent that our generation is insufficiently aware of the roots and meaning of the Christian message. Specialization in all lines of work has been found carried over into institutional religious life. Decisions belonging to all Christians have frequently fallen to a special class, the clergy. One of the cardinal aspects of the Prostestant interpretation of Christianity is thereby neglected.

Throughout these pages it is contended that the work of the church and the expression of the Christian faith will be evident in the major issues of our times. This involves a profound theological problem—the relationship of man to his fellow man and to God the Creator and Redeemer. But it is precisely because of our insufficient understanding of the way in which the Christian faith finds expression that the church and the Christian witness have been rendered less effective.

We have attempted to deal with only a few of the major issues in American life. Certain seemingly obvious ones, such as international relations and the use of power, have been omitted because they seem less suited for the kind of consideration here given. The treatment of each issue is brief and in no case all-inclusive. Rather, it attempts to suggest lines along which further study would be helpful.

The fundamental problems of this and every generation are theological in nature. But in our generation this fact has begun to assault us with increasing force. No longer can we keep our theological beliefs separate from the major issues of a society being drawn ever closer together. The vigor of the Christian witness will depend upon the layman's capacity for interpreting his faith in the significant areas of common life.

The nature of our theological beliefs determines the kind of society in which we live. It is our conviction about God—his existence or non-existence, his moral requirements, his design for individuals and society—which determines the kind of persons we are and the social order of which we are a part. There may be a tiny faction of humanity that works valiantly for justice and decency and is, at the same time, indifferent to any possibility of the existence of a deity. Such persons are of great worth, but their influence has been negligible as contrasted with those who maintain theological or antitheological beliefs.

This volume is primarily concerned with those who avow a belief in God and whose belief is influenced by the person of Jesus Christ. The decisions and actions that have shaped our times are largely the result of the actions of these people.

We know that there are discrepancies between what should be and what actually exists. The Christian religion has accomplished much in dignifying human life. (And when the term "Christian" is used, we recognize that its ethical requirements are, in most respects, identical with those of Judaism.) It must be apparent, however, to many Christians that a casualness or uncertainty about the implications of their faith has frequently resulted in its being undermined or even defeated. If some of us intend to be casual or indifferent, perhaps we may acknowledge it. But in honesty we must acknowledge that this commits us to the rejection of the very fundamentals of our faith. Few of us would be so forthright. More realistically, we suspect that the weaknesses tolerated in our society are instead the product of a watered-down, truncated, or soft-pedaled interpretation of the faith we have called Christian.

In periods of social upheaval and ferment men are pressed to look again at their heritage of theological foundations. The conscientious and thoughtful Christian does not wait for calamity to move him. He asks, "What does God require of me—now?" His convictions about God and God's own order are his ultimate—his most important —concerns. These are his theological convictions.

We have portrayed briefly in the first chapter some of the fundamental insights of the Christian faith as they relate to common life in society. Whereas our generation may have been reared to assume that we could adopt an attitude of "take it or leave it" in these matters of faith, it has become painfully apparent that this is a delusion. The social implications of our faith are presented not as something one might *add* to one's religion. They are integral to and inseparable from our faith. If there is a single strain running through the Old Testament, for example, it is the resounding cry that men and nations are responsible to God. In the New Testament the oneness of mankind is symbolized by the Cross, through which all men are united equally to accept sonship under a common Father. There is a unity, a wholeness, of life. Any attempt to reduce this or hide behind some limited personal piety is a perversion of the faith and brings destruction.

The Day of Judgment has been condescendingly regarded by modern men as a myth—spelled with a small "m." In its truest sense it is a Myth—spelled with a large "M," that is, a profound truth conveyed in symbolic language. The wisest men of our generation attest to the fact that that Day is here. When tanks and artillery are needed to escort a few children to school because of the pigmentation of their skin, when six million are burned or butchered for their religion, when a handful of men hold in their power the decision to obliterate all life on large portions of the globe, when half the world's population has come into a new political existence since World War II and many of them look hopefully to an antitheistic nation for clues to their personal and national salvation—the profound truth inherent in the Day of Judgment has been fulfilled. It is here. Thus, whether it is family life, international relations, activity on one's job, recreation, or any other phase of human life, decision and action reflect the true depths of our religion—or our theology.

In this mid-twentieth-century American life the theological foundations of Americans are affecting our national role in the competition for co-operation among nations both of the East and of the West.[1] The East-West battle is a contest of men's minds, and this contest arises out of a difference between fundamental beliefs held in the two nations which symbolize leadership in the contest.

Quickly some will retort that the issues between nations are political matters; they involve power politics and only secondarily or even remotely can be regarded as theological issues. On the contrary, it has become increasingly apparent in our national life, both within and without the borders of our nation, that all such decisions are founded upon our understanding of the nature of man and of the society which he composes. There are, it is true, large numbers of Christian people who would deny this connection between their personal Christian faith and the social implications of that faith. Religion is to them an intensely personal thing. It is their solemn conviction that godly and righteous people will conduct themselves in a way which reflects their godliness and righteousness. We believe this is true. The difficulty has been that people often have conceived godliness and righteousness in such limited forms that the terms have been deprived of their full meaning. And then, unwittingly perhaps, godliness and righteousness so narrowly conceived have served to encourage unrighteousness and injustice. It was to a condition not unlike this, perhaps, that Jesus was referring when he said, "The children of this world are in their generation wiser than the children of light." We are trying to discern the function of the children of light.

Without a doubt, it is not a coincidence that in those parts of the world where the Christian faith has laid its hold on the people the individual has been regarded as of greatest worth. Correspondingly, in those parts too, political institutions have arisen to protect man's work, and mechanical advancement has catered to his comfort. But what is generally termed "scientific progress" has not only created many of the issues which confront us personally and nationally but has also made necessary a reassessment of this relation between our religious beliefs and the life of our times.

CHAPTER I

CHRISTIAN FAITH AND
SOCIETY'S DIFFICULT
PROBLEMS

There is probably no more thrilling history outside the Bible and the history of Christian martyrdom than the founding of religiously grounded commonwealths in America. The story of America would indeed be poorer without the religious colonies and experiments in many parts of this country. Many who participated in them were fugitives from religious and civil persecution abroad. Their story has been told fully and fascinatingly in other places. We shall deal only with more recent developments.

THE SOCIAL GOSPEL

Between the Civil War and World War I there came into full vigor a movement known as the "Social Gospel." It attempted, among other things, to open the eyes of Americans to how religion was often used to anesthetize the consciences of Christians. It sought to acquaint people with the more inclusive concerns of Christianity as seen in the life of Jesus. Out of it grew a more careful study of Jesus' own life and his times. Correspondingly, it led to a more thorough analysis of our own time. It is noteworthy that in the last generation many of America's foremost analysts of society were products of this same movement.

The Social Gospel movement has been called America's most significant contribution to religious life and thought, and many American religious leaders are products of this movement. Foremost among the dynamic leaders who produced it was Walter Rauschenbusch, whose volume *Christianity and the Social Crisis* (1907) was probably the greatest contribution to the movement. He provided the zeal of a consecrated conscience and a brilliant intellect. Rauschenbusch, more than any other person, helped to provide a theological foundation and structure, without which no great movement has durability. His thought centered upon the idea of the Kingdom of God based upon Jesus' reference to the Kingdom as that goal toward which men would strive. By so doing, they would hope to achieve as much justice and decency as is possible here in our own time. The Social Gospel was closely identified with a scientific study of the Bible, paralleling in America a similar movement in Europe. It was felt that, if only men could comprehend the foundations which underlay both the ideas and the principal figures of the Old and New Testaments, they would appropriate those foundations themselves and go on from there toward the building of the Kingdom.

But then came a realization, already apparent to certain European theologians, that there were no formulas for the attainment of the Kingdom. Even a full knowledge of the social and economic life underlying the prophets and the life of Jesus would still leave men uninformed and inadequately acquainted with the Christian faith. Knowledge *about* Jesus was not enough. Applying the *principles* of Jesus still did not resolve the tough economic, political, and social issues. It is true that churchmen had succeeded in modifying some of the harshness of industrial life. They had, for example, taken a vigorous part in helping labor secure an eight-hour day in the steel industry. Many individual employers had sought to conduct their businesses on the basis of the Golden Rule or to ask themselves, "What would Jesus have me do?" But towering above all this was the realization that the fundamental issues of society were not to be resolved by any single formula.

A GREAT AWAKENING

Personal goodness had long been the objective of most religious life in America. But it was becoming apparent that personal goodness was an insufficient answer to the complex social issues of an industrial society. John Bennett has commented that the changing point in the complexion of American religious life can be dated with the publication of Reinhold Niebuhr's *Moral Man and Immoral Society* (1932). The title in itself carries a world of meaning. Individual goodness, even the desire "to be like Jesus," was not sufficient to cope with a theme as old as man's thought about himself and his society, namely, the problem of evil. Individual goodness or righteousness by itself was not enough. The evil in men who may have been exemplary husbands and fathers could still lead them into political action which debased and injured others.

Into this period came Hitler. A nation which could produce Luther could also, out of an inflamed nationalism, massacre six million Jews. A nation which had led the world in the scientific study of the life of Jesus could also demonstrate colossal inhumanity to man. Underlying this debauchery of the human spirit was more than ignorance; evil was something real and not merely the absence of the good. This unspeakable tragedy served to awaken man to the fact that the foundations of life are spiritual. Life may be good or it may be evil depending on the spiritual quality of those foundations. Modern man saw new meaning in the Apostle Paul's insistence:

For we have to struggle, not with enemies of flesh and blood, but with the hierarchies, the authorities, the master-spirits of this dark world, the spirit-forces of evil on high [Eph. 6:12].

9

From one who was not of the Christian faith comes what is perhaps the most telling testimony of the church's power to withstand evil. Albert Einstein said that at the time of the revolution in Germany, he looked to all who had claimed to uphold freedom—the universities, the newspapers, and individual writers—and found them all silenced. "Only the Church stood squarely across the path of Hitler's campaign for suppressing truth." It alone "had the courage and persistence to stand for intellectual truth and moral freedom."[1]

EUROPEAN AND AMERICAN DEVELOPMENTS

It must be added, however, that in a nation which for a period symbolized rejection of Christian values (Germany) there has come a mighty awakening of spiritual understanding. Recognition that the forces of evil can blank out good brought a deep searching on the part of nominal Christians as well as of scholars. Among the phenomena of this post–World War II period is to be recorded the development of the great laymen's movements in Europe, best symbolized, perhaps, by the *Kirchentag* in Germany. To these biennial five-day gatherings hundreds of thousands of Christians have been drawn for the purpose of discovering afresh the meaning of the Christian faith and for the deepening of spiritual life. Likewise, since World War II, the Laymen's Institutes have been growing in importance throughout Europe. To these centers for training and meditation come men and women of various professions, occupations, and interests to discern the meaning of the Christian faith for their particular type of work. American counterparts of such laymen's centers have come into being, and others are in process of formation. Presumably much more will be heard of this development within the next decade.

We have been calling attention, in the preceding paragraphs, to European manifestations of fresh interest in the Christian faith and its meaning for our current life. America has also shown evidences of awakening and of new directions. The National Council of the Churches of Christ in the United States of America in its manifold activities symbolizes the growth of American concern for a closer relationship between religion and the major issues of society. Three conferences on "The Church and Economic Life," the latest of which was held in Pittsburgh in 1956, reveal a deepening of understanding on the part of the Christian faith for our economic order. The same must be said for the first conference on "The Christian at His Daily Work," held in 1952 under similar auspices. Equally significant is the publication of the series of volumes on "Ethics and Economics of Society" produced under a grant from the Rockefeller Foundation and prepared by the Department of Church and Economic Life of what was originally the Federal Council of the Churches of Christ in America, which subsequently became the National Council of Churches. The import of this monumental undertaking lies in this same growing awareness that ethical issues in our economic life are rooted in theological foundations. To all this also must be added the pioneering work being done by agencies of the forward-looking denominations.

GOD

We have reiterated two things in the foregoing paragraphs: (1) that all actions inescapably reveal theological convictions about God and (2) that the Christian faith is inseparably related to the common life.

The study of theology is the study of ideas and convictions about God and the consequences of those ideas. Since some of the ablest minds in history have wrestled with this study and since the whole history of civilization has been influenced by it, no comprehensive or fully satisfying interpretation of such a study can be condensed in a few paragraphs. Our purpose is, rather, to attest to the fact that it is man's concern for the nature of God and what this means for his individual and social life which will determine his own life and that of his nation and his era.

We do not start our thinking with the idea of God. We begin with ourselves. But in moments of contemplation and serious awareness it becomes apparent that man is not the final end of all things. He has an origin, a source, a purpose, an end toward which his life is lived. Eventually, he asks, "What is man that thou art mindful of him?" Presumably at some time or other even the most casual and careless of persons asks the fundamental question: "Why am I here and how am I related to all the rest of the world of nature in which I am set?" It is at this point that the biblical insights bring illumination and yet deeper pondering. Man comes to realize that he is not set in solitariness, that he is a part of the human family. Again the meaning of the Apostle Paul's vivid illustration, likening a person to members of the body, takes on new meaning. Truly, no one part can say to another, "I do not need you" (I Cor. 12:21).

Behind all this, however, is the yet more penetrating insight that this dependence of man is not upon his brother or his neighbor or the world of nature; it is, rather, upon the source of life itself. Men have argued endlessly as to the nature of God. They will debate whether God interferes directly with man's affairs. They will ponder whether God suffers when man suffers, will wrestle with the question whether man's ultimate destiny is already determined for him or whether he has responsibility for his own acts and achieves salvation through his own ef-

12

forts. All these and countless other questions are of great importance.

Regardless of our opinions as to what God is or does, for the inheritor and participant in the Hebrew-Christian heritage there is one undeniable assumption. Simply stated, it is the sentence in the Twenty-fourth Psalm, "The earth is the Lord's." Such an insight and others like it in biblical literature constitute a revolutionary demand upon the life of man. It is of a piece with the wisdom of the first sentence in the Bible, "In the beginning God created. . . ." These statements and the entire content of the scriptures point to this single fact: all life is of God's creation, and man is ultimately beholden to this source of his being.

Man cannot possibly encompass or comprehend the full nature of God. We can simply live our lives with the realization that we are living in God himself. He is, therefore, literally closer to us than breathing, nearer than hands or feet. That we cannot describe God should be no source of frustration. How can man describe what is itself the source of description? Understandably, men have conceived of God in personal terms. But God is more than person. Paul Tillich has suggested that God is not so much a being as the very ground of all being. Truly, "it is He that hath made us" and we are His.

CHRIST

Whatever divisions or disagreement there may be as to the nature of God, the Christian world is in substantial agreement that Jesus Christ reveals to man what God is like. For centuries men have wrestled with such issues as whether or not Jesus was identical with God himself or was human like other men. Presumably this argument will never cease. Sects and religious movements have arisen around these differences. Reducing our understanding of the nature of Jesus Christ to some kind of a lowest com mon denominator, however, is an unsatisfactory method of resolving the dilemma.

It is the point of view of this book and of a substantial portion of Christians that Jesus was both human and divine. In the person of Christ, God entered into the human scene in a distinct and unique fashion. In his life among men he was completely human, even as we are. In the act of self-sacrifice which led to his death he exemplified the supreme sacrifice on behalf of his fellow men. But in so doing he revealed the way in which God gives himself for mankind. What followed the death of Jesus is entirely of God's doing. His act in the Resurrection is the specific intervention of God in the human scene, giving assurance of the continuance of life in God himself.

The claim of Jesus Christ upon men, then, is not merely the claim of a good life, however exemplary. It is rather the claim which God makes upon us for having shared with us this revelation of himself. This revelation God makes eternally convincing because of what he himself did with the life of one whom we know in history as Jesus Christ.

In no way does this realization of God's act in the person of Jesus minimize Jesus' human side. On the contrary, it glorifies it and makes it more significant for the living of human life. The significance of Jesus' humanity serves but to make the more meaningful his witness to God's intention for mankind.

Scholars have labored to present the honest facts of Jesus' life. We know that the situation in which a person lives determines in a large measure the kind of life he lives. Understandably, then, searchers have attempted to encompass as fully as possible the circumstances in which Jesus lived his comparatively brief life on this earth. Albert Schweitzer's *Quest of the Historical Jesus* (1926) is symbolic of many such attempts to get at the historically veri-

fiable facts about Jesus' earthly life. Such a study will presumably never end. We can never know too much about
the actual facts of his life. Regardless of how much we
may learn, however, it is wholly unlikely that these facts
will counteract the other side of Jesus' identity—God's
intervention into the human scene and all that it means.

Out of Jesus' very human experience emerged the parables and narratives revealing so vividly his intimate knowledge of practical and ordinary life. As men have sought to
explore the meaning of those parables and human experiences, their depths become increasingly apparent. In every
instance they were more than a description of a human
situation. They pointed to a dependence and an obligation. In every instance they symbolized the relation between God and man, man's dependence upon God for
physical and spiritual nourishment.

The ethical demands of Jesus have been portrayed in his
parables and in his own personal associations with those
about him. Laws have been formulated and their enforcement fortified on the assumption that they were required
by the evidence in the life of Jesus. Many such attempts
have led to trouble. Part of the difficulty stemmed from
the obvious fact that the authority of Jesus was not held
in the same esteem by everyone. But even more serious is
the assumption that Jesus' injunctions can be made to
apply to all specific conditions and situations. It is at this
point that misgiving has arisen over the validity of Jesus'
requirements, at least as they are interpreted by modern
men.

A key to an understanding of the change taking place
in our beliefs about Jesus' requirements lies in this change
in our conviction about Jesus himself. Just as scholars and
all religious-minded searchers have sought to comprehend
this relation between Christianity and social issues, many
men have attempted to discover in the scriptures what

came to be called "the principles of Jesus." They presumed that certain formulas could be applied which would guarantee a Christian outcome. Charles M. Sheldon wrote his famous book *In His Steps* (1896) around the idea of a person attempting to live his life for a given period as Jesus would have him do, or according to Jesus' principles. It was a noble idea and made a profound impression on a whole generation. An indication of the popularity of the idea is the fact that probably more copies of Sheldon's book have been sold than any other book printed in America with the exception of the Bible.

But two world wars and the rise of totalitarianism, in the form of fascism and communism, have disabused men's minds of the thought that the principles of Jesus were "sufficient," at least in the sense in which that word is used. Jesus as the Christ involves something deeper than a set of principles. He reveals in startling and compelling fashion the very nature of man himself and of his relationship to God.

LOVE

From the record of Jesus' life and sayings come incidents which reflect the deeper meaning of man's relationship to God and to his fellow men. One of those is the parable of the Good Samaritan. Jesus is asked, "Who is my neighbor?" His reply is couched in terms of a man in need to whom love was shown in the form of tangible assistance. Hospitals, schools, rehabilitation centers, and all manner of beneficial agencies have been constructed around this parable. Underlying the story, however, is something touching life at all levels. What is involved here is not merely a single person helping another individual. A whole plan of human society and its ultimate dependence is symbolized in this gripping story. The temptation to limit neighborliness to individuals close at hand

16

has often obscured for the church and its people the fuller meaning of that parable. What the Good Samaritan did was to express the fulness of love on behalf of another individual. In this act he revealed the way in which God shares his love with all men. But as George Thomas has pertinently commented, "Love of neighbor cannot be confined to relationship between persons, but must also be part of the collective relationship between classes, races, and nations in the form of justice."[2]

Love that is limited to the "in-group"—those already well known and intimate—is a much abbreviated love. In fact it may not be love at all. It can be a form of selfishness. The heart of the entire biblical message lies in the Good Samaritan story. There God's love is given freely and not on some equal trading basis. Neither is love limited in its application. The implication is very plain that, if men would merit the love God shows to them, their own response can hardly be less.

But the expression of love toward one's neighbor does not convey to us the full nature of the person of Jesus Christ. His meaning for mankind is infinitely more inclusive. The story does reveal, however, how impossible it is to express the Christian faith in any kind of formula or to limit the meaning of Christ to any set of principles, however "Christian" their labels may be. It is to this more inclusive meaning that Paul appeals when he urges that men "have this mind in you which was in Christ Jesus," he urges men to understand the mind of him who reflected in himself the love of God toward man and to understand man's necessity for a corresponding expression to his neighbor. Only thus can man return the love given to him. It is in the person of Jesus Christ that men see God's love illustrated. His example is constantly available.

Preceding the parable of the Good Samaritan and giving rise to it was the question, "Master, what command is the greatest in the Law?" Jesus replied:

"You must love the Lord your God with your whole heart, your whole soul, and your whole mind." That is the great, first command. There is a second like it: "You must love your neighbor as you do yourself." These two commands sum up the whole of the Law and the Prophets [Matt. 22:36–40].

Love of God and love of neighbor are inseparably coupled. Love of neighbor in Jesus' thinking can be genuine love only if it is as considerate of one's neighbor as it is of one's self. Here, of course, is a highly involved issue. Philosophers and psychologists may deal with the question of self-love and the extent to which one can be mindful of another and still sufficiently protective of one's self. Jesus did not get involved in this complex discussion. People who have not lost capacity for reason and consideration of others cannot but be aroused to a new appreciation of the meaning of love when it is put in his terms. But this is no mere formula. One's love for one's self is not a measured matter— it cannot be closely described and analyzed. We do know, however, that it is present.

Here, then, is the test of the integrity and sincerity of one's religion, at least in the Hebrew-Christian tradition: that one's love for God is measured by one's love for neighbor and the check on one's love for neighbor is the appraisal of it against one's love for one's self.

The word which the Apostle Paul uses for love in the same sense in which Jesus reveals it is "agape." Love has come to have many meanings, and the sense in which Jesus uses it has been grossly distorted. Love of husband and wife, or parents and children, or friend and friend may be a part of the idea of love in the sense of agape, but it is not identical with it. There are other terms to express those various relationships. Agape, however, is the complete self-giving of one person for another in the same manner that God gives of himself to man.

Love, thus, is not a simple formula for human society; it is that toward which men strive and against which our limited human capacities are constantly measured. A loving parent desires to give his children the best things and experiences it is possible for him to give. All the while, however, he realizes that giving to his children may cause deprivation to some others. Privileges for those we love must often be bought at the expense of others likewise in need. Herein lies the eternal dilemma of the good and loving person. And the situation confronting parents likewise confronts organizations and nations. Even at this moment America wishes to utilize her vast surpluses of grain for other nations whose people are hungry. The act of doing so, however, under the economic arrangements now prevailing could actually bring disaster to producers in other parts of the world. Obviously a desire to live a life of love or to act upon a basis of love requires more than good intention. There are complicated and technical aspects which are not resolved by mere well-wishing. Nevertheless, there is so vast a realm within which love can be expressed that we need not be blocked either by real or imagined technical difficulties, impressive though they be. Love as a force in human life is not to be ruled out as a realistic option or instrument of personal and social well-being. We turn briefly, therefore, to some of the means actually available for implementing love.

LOVE IN PRACTICE

As has been asserted above in many different ways, there is no set of formal requirements governing individual and social conduct which can be attributed to the New Testament. Neither is there a formula for Christian action. There is, however, a powerful compulsion toward it.

Despite insistence from many sources that the Christian faith is primarily a personal religion, there is nothing in the summation of the Scriptures to support that limited conception. The entire history of our faith is steeped in its social implications. Justification for a religion that is merely personal is not to be found in the Bible. Difficult though it may seem to state precise ways of expressing love for God in one's relations with one's neighbor, are there not an infinite number of ways in which this may be done? Democracy itself has aided mightily in facilitating love in society. Curtailing the opportunities for injustice and demanding that there be equal opportunity for the development of the self has been perhaps the greatest aid to love in the common life of mankind. The existence of the political system known as democracy is not itself an expression of love, but it makes possible a greater achievement or fulfilment of love.

Another achievement of democracy is justice. One of the most quoted aphorisms of our day is Reinhold Niebuhr's "Man's capacity for justice makes democracy possible; but man's inclination to injustice makes democracy necessary."[3] Though justice and democracy are not in themselves to be regarded as ultimate expressions of love, they are, nevertheless, means for facilitating it. The inescapable fact is that there is no such thing as love in social relations and in society generally that is not also founded upon justice. So it can be insisted that justice is love in action. William Temple remarked that there is no need to "bleat fatuously" about love when what is needed is plain justice. "The point is not that love is unimportant in dealing with social problems, the point is that love is not love but sentimental talk unless it manifests itself practically in seeking justice for all."[4]

In the following chapters this conviction about justice as love in action underlies the exposition and exploration of each theme. In no instance does love dictate the blue-print for a social policy. Nevertheless, in almost every instance, there are issues involving justice. Love of God and neighbor require as a very minimum the recognition of the issues and a sensitivity to the demands of justice.

THE CHURCH

The Christian faith is no solitary affair. Though one's religion may be tested in part by what one does in solitary moments, human beings are not isolated and independent units. Actually we are what we are because of our membership in the human company. From this fact stems the very existence of the church.

The church is, among other things, a fellowship. It is a fellowship of those who seek to give their first loyalty to God as we know him in Jesus Christ. Through this fellowship Christ's spirit, which we call the "Holy Spirit," finds expression. This is not to say that God has no other means of influencing his world. It is rather to confess that in fellowship men and women who have sensed God's sovereignty seek ways of discovering and expressing what this means.

Though we may be quite aware that our lives have been shaped and determined by our association with others, the extent of that influence we have, in all probability, never fully appraised. It may be that our religious training and the society in which we were brought up have accentuated our sense of individualism. In some measure this is a rejection of the tribal conformity and the complete domination of life by society that once prevailed. To a considerable degree the church and religious customs fostered this sense of uniformity. Protestantism and Western culture generally, however, gave a new impetus to the individual and his capacity for independence. It would seem now that the pendulum has swung back again to a more realistic position wherein account is taken of man's interdependence.

The Christian understanding of life assumes the interdependence of all men. Jesus points to this fact in a simple but unmistakable fashion. He refers to God as "Our Father." Here is recognition of an elemental truth. Though social science has accepted the unity of society as a cornerstone of its discipline, it is fundamentally a religious idea. Only of late have we come to recognize that the biblical understanding of society is correct. Where men have been led to act on a different assumption, lives have been warped and broken.

The Christian church, thus, starts with the assumption that all men are children of the same Father. In fulfilling the meaning of that assumption we have in the person of Jesus the example of what God desires in human relationships. The church, therefore, seeks to exemplify in its fellowship the manner and the spirit of Christ.

We have been speaking of the church both as an organization and as a fellowship bound together by a common commitment. For the moment, however, it is the organization with which we are concerned. It is almost axiomatic that organizations get in the way of their own fundamental purpose. Rare indeed is that organization which constantly seeks to review its intention and deliberately re-adapts itself to changing needs in the light of its purpose. The simple fact is that fellowships which take on organizational form seek to become exclusive and to serve their own ends, forgetting often the original purpose of their founders. This, to put it bluntly, is what has frequently happened to the institution of the church. Its members, too, forget the fundamental purpose for which the institution came into being. The fault lies not in the institution or the organization itself. Organizations and institutions are necessary. They make possible united action. They carry the body of ideas and traditions by which the young are first informed and through which they grow in understanding of beliefs and traditions. But the ever present problem of an institution is to implement its basic purposes and to find new ways of increasing its effectiveness. This is the pre-eminent function of the institution we know as the church.

The church, thus, is seen both as a truth to be expressed and as an institution to foster that truth. It is the body of Christ in the sense that it does God's work as Christ would do it among men. A metallurgist in a class once conducted by the author spontaneously burst out with the observation, "Why the church is the Christian faith, isn't it—its belief and its action?" This was good insight. Yes, the church is God working among men through his Holy Spirit. It is also the institution dedicated to facilitating his work. These two facts are intertwined and inseparable. Any belittling of one brings diminution to the other. A large portion of the church's dilemma in our generation stems from a misunderstanding of this connection.

COMMUNITY

What do we mean by community? A study of sociological definitions turned up more than ninety different ones.[5] Most of them presumed a definite geographical space, a location with people related to it. But there are other uses of the term. Frequently reference is made to a professional community such as "the medical community," to a nationality group such as "the Italian community," or to "the community of nations." Again, a religious community is presumed to include members of a particular faith. Obviously, the term has many uses.

Here, however, we are using the term "community" in reference both to a local area and to society as a whole. An individual church's concern for its own local community derives from the church's concern for the community as an idea and a conviction—in all society.

Underlying the use of the term is an assumption that men are bound together in mutual obligation and dependence upon one another and upon God. The local church seeks to demonstrate this fact in the area it knows best. As part of the church at large, it joins with other local churches to implement God's love in society as a whole or to achieve community.

Whole libraries have been written describing the church's efforts and accomplishments in the achievement of community. A few brief references pertaining to certain present trends, however, will suffice. In 1937, as the clouds of war were gathering and the tragic consequences of economic failures were still everywhere apparent, there was held in Oxford, England, a conference of church people from all over the world. The theme of that conference was "Church, Community, and State." Primarily the conference was concerned with the basic message of the Christian faith as it applied to economic and political life. Here for the first time on a major scale the church sought to deal with the problem of community in its fuller sense. Oxford marked a milestone in the history of the church and its social concern. Dr. C. L. Patijn, a lawyer and a member of the Dutch delegation to the United Nations, commented that the Oxford conference established the trend of Christian thinking in the following years and represented "a tremendous forward step in Christian thinking."[6]

In 1948, another world war having intervened, the Amsterdam Assembly of the World Council of Churches attempted to further the work done at Oxford. Here emerged the term, originated primarily by J. H. Oldham, "the responsible society." Dr. Patijn says this term indicates society's concern for the protection of all the victims of the technological age—the unemployed or the persecuted peoples and the underdeveloped nations of the world. At the same time the term expresses the church's concern for the individual in a large society, for the individual's ability to be a free, responsible person in social, political, and private life.[7] In an even more definite sense at the Amsterdam Assembly, thus, the work of the church in creating community constitutes its basic concern.

Six years later at Evanston, Illinois, the World Council met again. Another war had been fought, a cold war was in progress, and a minor recession had given the jitters to a great many people. It was becoming apparent to an ever increasing number of individuals that the root of man's dilemma could not be reached or affected by good intentions or by turning the back on situations. More and more responsible Christians were realizing that the achievement of community involves responsible action. A glance at the subjects and the reports of the various sections of the Evanston conference vividly bears this out. Among the themes dealt with were: "The Responsible Society and a World Perspective"; "The Christian in the Struggle for World Community"; "Resolutions on Religious Liberty"; "The Church amid Racial and Ethnic Tensions."

The time for well-meaning pronouncements has passed. A church content merely to extol principles has in a considerable measure abdicated and defaulted. It has lost its capacity for leadership. The times require prophetic action, and the area of prophetic action is the determination to achieve an ever larger measure of the Christian community. This is the task of the church both at large and in its local setting. A church thus capable of inspiring and leading such action will portray the church triumphant and, incidentally, will not lack adherents.

THE CHRISTIAN REQUIREMENT

Christianity, we must frequently be reminded, is not a set of beliefs. It is a way of life, a way of life based upon a conviction concerning the ultimate purposes of life. But purposes cannot be maintained aloof from real life and its very ordinary contacts. Realistic contacts with life confront all but the most insensitive men with the fact of their involvement in the whole fabric of humanity. There is, thus, actually no avoiding responsibility for participation. To take no responsibility is, in one sense, to assume responsibility for permitting others to shape our destinies. This lesson we have been learning to our sorrow in recent years. Not to act, therefore, is to act unwittingly.

The church has always been deeply concerned with giving expression to its social message. Its heritage of social action goes back to the time of Hebrew prophecy and is seen in the life of Jesus, in the church of the New Testament and of the Middle Ages, in the Reformation, and in more modern movements. It is foolish, and perhaps hypocritical, to deny that religion is involved in political life. The gospel gives no hint that a man may be a steward of God only in selected activities that he calls "religious."[8]

But how, we ask, can one be certain that his action is in conformity with the spirit of Christ when there are so many alternatives, so many unforeseen consequences? Obviously, the answer is that we cannot know which solution is absolutely right, which plan most surely accords with God's will. We do, however, know whether our own intentions and actions are based upon the assumption of God's sovereignty in human life and history. We know whether we have sought to respond to a living God whose gift of grace is available to men honestly seeking to make decisions dedicated to him.

It is in the making of these decisions that the community of faith undergirds us. By ourselves we know we may be insufficient to judge wisely or act responsibly. The Christian places his decision and action before the whole tradition of his faith and before the judgment of like-minded fellow servants. All decisions presume standards. They may range from a mere desire for personal gain to utter selflessness and the desire for the good of all men. If we sincerely seek the truest of answers, we may with reason and expectancy bring our concern to the prayerful considerations of the household of faith. Thus, when men are willing to submit their decisions both to the best insights of their faith and to the practical judgment of other sincere and informed men, there is reasonable assurance that God's purposes are furthered.

The possibility that influences and intentions other than those of God are being fostered confronts us with another fundamental element in Christian thought and decision. It is the fact of human sin. Though our chief interest in these pages lies in the nature of the Christian faith and the way it meets some of the major issues of our time, we would default on our responsibility if no consideration were given to the fact of sin. Educated or "emancipated" people have seemingly found less use for this idea or condition in our generation than have some of our forebears. A false and distorted use of the term has brought it into disrepute. Now once again, however, it is becoming apparent that the condition which is included in the original meaning of the term is something very real. Without it there is no adequate description of what prevails when men conduct their affairs independently or in defiance of God.

Sin, then, is whatever alienates men from God. It may be open defiance, but more likely it is the naïve or arrogant assumption that of ourselves we can determine what is best. Refusal, therefore, to submit our purposes and in-

THE RESPONSIBLE CHRISTIAN

tentions to God's judgment is in itself a form of sinfulness and idolatry, an alienation from God. It is a part of man's sinfulness. We have needed a fresh reminder of the human tendency to "go it alone," giving lip service to our faith where convenient. We have been wont to attribute sinfulness primarily to "the world rulers of this present darkness" while overlooking, perhaps, the subtle but very real tendency to sinfulness in our own alienation from God.

Active participation in the attempt to further God's work in human society has thus both a positive and a negative aspect. The positive lies in the conscious desire to direct our action in conformity with the known and discoverable purposes of our Creator in whose life we live. The negative aspect is the reluctance to accept the history of our faith and the judgment of sincere followers of Christ in favor of our own desires and intentions. These are our alternatives as Christians. What we have been calling "social action" is the testing ground of the Christian faith. "By their fruits ye shall know them."

We turn now to some of the most trying problems of our times. To them we would bring the resources of our faith. We realize that all these issues involve highly technical decisions, that no single Christian solution awaits. They are, however, in every instance basically spiritual problems. Any progress toward their solution, therefore, hinges upon a comprehension of their spiritual nature. But also our attempts to find solutions to them constitute one of the infallible tests of our Christian faith.

CHAPTER II

ECONOMIC LIFE

The frontiers of religious life for our times are in the realm of economics. And just as truly can it be said that the frontiers of economics are in the realm of religion.

It has become apparent to a substantial number of businessmen that the forces with which they are dealing and the decisions they must make are finally determined in relation to values outside of what is considered economics and outside of the business in which they are engaged. Similarly can it be said that economics as a science depends upon ideas and values not found in the operation of economic "laws" themselves.

The history of American business life is enriched with the biographies of men who have been convinced that religion and ethics cannot be divorced from business practices. No one could adequately appraise the impact on American business life by dedicated and deeply religious men and women. Their personal witness has made a profound impression. But it is not with the personal dedication and Christian commitment that we are here primarily concerned; it is rather with the economic order in which good and less than good individuals must live their lives and earn their daily bread.

In the last analysis, it is true, all decisions are made by individuals, but the *system* within which they make their decisions may extend farther than the decisions themselves. Christianity has placed large emphasis upon the *quality* of individuals, with the assumption that they in turn would make the system what it ought to be. By now it has become apparent that our personal decisions are made within a given economic system and that men must seek to influence the larger setting as well as make just and honorable personal decisions.

The reasons why righteous, God-loving men and women have failed to comprehend the importance of this larger setting and their relationship to it are many and complex. They have to do with the development of our whole industrial life, with the intellectual freedom that came with the Renaissance, and with the political systems that arose in Europe and America as a result of religious and intellectual freedom. All this is a fascinating study by itself. Perhaps nowhere is this explained and interpreted more comprehensively than by Richard H. Tawney in his classic volume, *Religion and the Rise of Capitalism* (1926).

Fortunately, in America as well as elsewhere in the world, there is a substantial company of people who have come to realize the inseparableness of religion, ethics, and economics. They know that the Christian faith is applicable to every phase of a person's life, that ethics are the modes of conduct which grow out of one's religion, and that economics, the area in which one deals with the goods of life, provides an unfailing test of one's real religion or faith.

Chester Barnard, former president of the New Jersey Bell Telephone Company and of the Rockefeller Foundation, is one of this growing company of thoughtful businessmen who know that economic decisions are based upon ethical values. He and others of this newer type of sensitive and informed business leaders have realized that religiously motivated ethical ideas are either all-important or they are of no importance. The evidence points to the fact that they are of supreme importance. Then why has this been so little understood or accepted in practice? Fortunately, Mr. Barnard was in a position to do something about it. He and his colleagues on the board of the Rockefeller Foundation offered to make Foundation money available for a thorough study of this misunderstood or insufficiently understood area of our life. Out of

this interest has grown the most significant study ever conducted on the relation between religion, ethics, and economics. The results are published in seven volumes produced under the auspices of the Department of Church
and Economic Life of what is now the National Council
of Churches of Christ in the U.S.A., with Charles P. Taft
as chairman of the department and Cameron P. Hall as
executive director.

Protestantism has no papal encyclicals constituting the
final authority for the judgment of its people in matters
of great decision. No single voice can, therefore, speak for
all Protestants, and we are glad that such is the case. However, this presumes that a large body of people are as thoroughly informed and as dedicated to the truth as the company of those who formulate the encyclicals issued by the
Pope. Protestants rightfully pride themselves on the fact
that their consciences, informed by and dedicated to God's
holy will, constitute the ultimate basis of action. But obviously the key to this situation lies in the extent to which
those consciences have sought to be informed by every possible revelation of God's will. Christians will therefore
make use of all resources that will throw light on economic
decisions. As Protestantism has fostered free and uninhibited search for the truth in its educational institutions,
it must depend upon its people to apply the fruits of their
search and wisdom to each issue confronting men. In hu-
mility we must confess that this we have not done. The
present confusion in the relationship of religion, ethics,
and economics is all too vivid an illustration of our failure.

The consequences of our unwillingness or ignorance in
using what we know about the connection between ethics
and economics have caught up with us. The scope of the
East-West tension is but one illustration. The smoldering
conflict between America and Russia is to be explained finally in just those terms. More will be said of this later. Many

of the ablest historians and analysts of today have contended that our failure to apply what we know about ethics and economic life provides the basis for the conflagration that has swept over the Far East. Likewise it must be said that all the issues with which our present volume is concerned—civil rights, conservation of national resources, labor-management relations, or any of the others—are grounded in this problem of ethics and economic life.

The church has not always made clear its full relationship to this problem. But, increasingly, the church's concern is coming to the fore. The Amsterdam Conference of the World Council of Churches (1948) and, likewise, the Evanston conference (1954) sought to define what is meant by a "responsible society." Implied in the patiently wrought statements of the commission in both these conferences is a relevance of the church to the total order of society. The use of the word "responsible" implies that there is a source to which man is responsible. It implies a higher reference than obligation to one's own community or nation.

SOME MAJOR DECISIONS FOR AMERICAN CHRISTIANS

With no attempt to be inclusive or to present a complete catalogue of economic issues, there follows a series of brief statements concerning some of the areas in which decisions are required. There are, of course, many others. In them, too, any action will be posited upon values deemed fundamental. Confronted with major decisions, the Christian must ask the basic questions.

1. It is only a relatively short time since the period when it was assumed that poverty was the result of laziness. Now we know that a part of the costs of our kind of industrial society is broken homes, delinquency, fatherless children and working mothers, and the inability of the "great fam-

ily" (aunts, uncles, grandparents, and other kinfolk) to
provide. One of the phrases around which much heat is
generated is "welfare state." At this point our favorable inclination toward the Good Samaritan and our misgiving
about the increasing power of the state come into conflict.
Propaganda slogans only confuse the issue. Deeply imbedded in our culture is a conviction that human needs
must be met. The extent of those needs confronts us with
providing solutions more comprehensive than personal
charity makes possible. Our Christian faith and ethics call
for more than sentiment or propaganda.

With our expanding economy it has been possible to
provide a wide range of security measures for the aged, unemployed, dependent, handicapped, etc. But there are still
many not covered by the various forms of federal and state
insurance. Agricultural labor, migrant workers, and employees of plants hiring too few to qualify are illustrations.
Thus, some who most need security are deprived of it.
They lack union organizations to work for their interests.

2. Schools bursting with children and operating on double and even triple shifts may be undermining our prized
public education system. But the source of taxes and the
freedom or lack of freedom of families to move where they
choose is determining whether or not children shall have
a satisfactory education. Many people resist further encroachment of the federal government upon the administration of individual states and therefore are opposed to
federal aid for schools. Is education an individual or a state
matter, or does it affect the welfare of the nation as a
whole? There is much reason to suspect that the attempt
to dictate the quality and content of teaching within the
public schools is closely related to the economic philosophy of persons who are thus seeking to limit the freedom
of schools and education in general. Obviously, the prerogatives of communities are at stake here. But also there is

THE RESPONSIBLE CHRISTIAN

the prior question of the obligation on the part of adults to facilitate all possible growth of the young into full maturity. It seems reasonable to infer that some of the opposition to free and full education comes at the hands of those who themselves lack spiritual and intellectual maturity.

3. Surpluses acquired during the post–World II period have provided one of the darkest clouds on the American economic horizon. Yet, while surpluses accumulate, a very large part of the world's population continues to go hungry. To many the solution seems simple—give the excess foodstuffs away. In contrast to the amount of money poured into war materials the cost of giving away our food surpluses would be slight. But in this process there is always the danger of wrecking even such economic stability as other nations have achieved. Obviously, the issue is not simple. But the very fact that America possesses the surpluses while other nations are in dire need serves only to aggravate the relation between America and the other nations. Like all the other problems dealt with here, this is one which involves both technical understanding and a foundation in Christian concern.

4. Such terms as "mixed economy," "capitalism," and "socialism" are charged with emotion; their use renders thoughtful consideration impossible for many people. When, in the Amsterdam conference, both laissez faire capitalism and communism were condemned, many church people in America were incensed over the linking of the two in condemnation, despite the fact that there has never prevailed in America a laissez faire capitalism. Our post-office system, road system, income tax, pure-food laws, and various forms of business regulations all reflect our disavowal of laissez faire capitalism. There are few people who would do away with any of these controls. But it is true we do not have an adequate name to describe the type

of economy now operating in this country. Just as an Eisenhower administration eliminated none of the major changes of the Truman-Roosevelt periods, so the conservative government in England did away with none of the major economic changes effected by the Labor government. Were those changes perhaps so close to fundamental human need that partisan considerations were secondary?

5. Closely related to the type of economic system Christians can approve is the issue of the profit motive and the profit system. The word "profit" has become almost a sacred term. But obviously, if profit were the only consideration, chaos would result. It has been convincingly shown that profit is not always the primary consideration in work. There are other incentives just as important, or more so: quality of workmanship, comradeship, esteem of one's fellow workers, etc. We operate within a profit system, but this does not mean that profit is the sole concern of the individual.[1]

6. Christians have shied away from the term "power" and what it implies. But decisions in government and in group life are very largely based upon power, the power of those seeking a particular advantage or end. Government is conducted by blocs. Every good as well as every evil thing that has occurred in our representative government has stemmed from a pressure exercised in behalf of individuals or groups. There has been a temptation on the part of some good Christians to close their eyes while others take up the collection. Power in itself is not evil. Both moral and physical power can be utilized for great good. In a complex modern society those organizations and individuals that have made an intelligent and morally persuasive case for their objectives and have been sufficiently diligent to rally the support of righteous folk are most likely to accomplish their ends.

7. Everyone is for international trade. When it comes, however, to the specific terms of trade, the tariff arrangements pinch someone. With the world becoming increasingly interdependent, collaboration and concession is indispensable to economic well-being. But this is more than mutual back-scratching. It presumes a realization of common dependence and destiny.

8. Traditionally in our religious heritage work has been good. But some kinds of work and some degrees of work can be damaging. The twelve-hour day in the steel industry was wrecking family life and throwing lives on the scrap heap prematurely. Christian people acting concertedly protested this desecration of human life and demanded that it cease. The Christian ethical demand was right. Religious people have vehemently protested child labor. Likewise, employment of impressionable youth in demoralizing places is a source of deep concern.

Many types of employment are producing a large number of individuals who, eager for status, recognition, and security, aim to achieve the accepted standards of success as early as possible. Because in increasing numbers people seemingly must find employment in ever enlarging companies, the strain involved in going up the ladder increases. Ethical conduct is frequently deprecated. Undoubtedly, business organizations are becoming increasingly responsive to public interest, and the larger they become the more sensitive they must be to public attitude. Nevertheless, the very fact of greater size makes for added pressure to reach the top. Wives as well as husbands are involved. The effects of the straining process are felt by families and communities as well as by the persons directly participating.

In such a time as ours, when physical labor declines and the amount of time spent in actual manual or clerical work grows less, there is a corresponding concern for the

36

wide use of the added leisure now available to many people in the industrialized portions of the world. The full significance of automation has not yet become apparent. Our concern is for the opportunities for creative expression and the fulfilment of personality. This is a religious concern, not "merely" an economic matter.

9. Finally and perhaps most important of all in present-day American life are the consequences of our economy of abundance for religious life. Never before in human history has any nation known the state at which this nation has arrived. Most people actually and all people potentially have enough to eat, to wear, and to shelter them. This may be a greater burden upon the human soul than living in a measure of deprivation. The test of our fundamental humanity as children of God lies immediately before us.

SOURCE OF OUR CHRISTIAN CONCERN FOR ECONOMIC LIFE

Many of the issues mentioned in the preceding paragraphs have been the concern of thoughtful people in the Hebrew-Christian tradition for at least 3,000 years. Religion and economic life have always been closely related. The Hebrew prophets were concerned about poverty and those dispossessed because of the monopoly of land (Isa. 5:8). The sabbatical year and the year of jubilee were designed to provide for the disadvantaged in the seventh year and for the return of all land to its original owners at the end of the forty-ninth year, implying that land belongs to God. The Hebrew prophets contended that their contemporaries had disregarded these requirements so flagrantly that disaster was inevitable.

Jesus' ethical teachings are replete with suggestions concerning the limitations on our possessions and the unimportance of treasures laid up on earth, admonishing the wise use of one's money and possessions in a stewardship capacity. He reminded men that they could not serve two masters. Preoccupation with goods and possessions dulled the capacity for fuller spiritual understanding. All goods as well as life itself were subject to the law of love, which takes precedence over all else and gives meaning to everything that one has and does.

In the early Christian community, we are told, "they that believed were together and had all things in common; and they sold their possessions and goods and parted them to all according as any man had need" (Acts 2:44-45). Economic life was subordinate to the glorious era which awaited the faithful.

In the life of the Middle Ages the highest ideal was the recognition that possessions and life itself should be administered to the glory of God as the giver of them. The result of this attitude, according to Tawney, is that ". . . economic interests are subordinate to the real business of life, which is salvation, and that economic conduct is one aspect of personal conduct, upon which, as on other parts of it, the rules of morality are binding."[2]

When the Protestant Reformation became a reality it had to deal with economic life more directly than the Roman Catholic faith had required previously. In fact, it was the emergence of new developments in economic life that stimulated desire for new political realignments, particularly in Germany. These in turn provided encouragement for the religious reforms led by Martin Luther. Thus it was natural that Protestantism should adapt itself more readily to the new economic order. But to give it direction still remained a fundamental problem. To Luther, love provided the primary inner motivation and served as the guide for all economic activity. The economic order was to be brought under the power of the state, but good men, Luther believed, could be counted on to administer the state wisely. Calvin, on the other hand, was unwilling to trust as much to what love might dictate to men in their conduct. In the light of what Calvin and his followers believed were God's intentions for society, a model order was established after Old Testament patterns in the city of Geneva, Switzerland. Industrious activity and economic gain were regarded as indications of God's favor. Man's responsibility entered at the point of using the fruits of his labor and thrift after the manner of a faithful steward. Quite obvious is the extent to which this conviction of Calvin has colored the economic life and thought in the countries influenced by the Protestant Reformation, particularly England and the United States.

As the industrial revolution began to flower in England its consequences were disturbing to a people who had been trained in both Old and New Testament lore. The blighted lives of the great cities belied the biblical idea of man's dignity and of his work before God. There emerged a dynamic protest born of a biblical-Christian heritage and of a political freedom which was itself religiously founded. From it came a movement of Christian socialism which sought to free men from the bondage into which an exploited economic system was thrusting them. The British Labor party and the liberal wing of other political groups in Great Britain have been strongly influenced by Christian socialist pioneers.

In America, where the industrial revolution was fast taking hold and creating a new economic and industrial giant, there was arising also a movement among religiously sensitive people. Its purpose was to temper the barbarities and brutalities of a raw economic system. Here it became known as the Social Gospel. The very name indicates the truncated and partial interpretation given to the gospel at that time. Obviously, there is no such thing as a separation between the personal and the social gospel. However, a nation of people raised upon a strictly individualistic religion of personal salvation was unequipped to cope with the vast social forces shaping and often misshaping human lives. The industrial and economic evils in America began to reach proportions no longer to be overlooked. The tide of immigration, the concentration of economic power, the destruction of competitors by special political privilege, the rise of child labor—these and many more evils—touched the consciences of American church people.

Many of the first students of social life in this country were ministers, products of a gospel which would not allow men to be at ease where life was being blighted. Sociology departments of American colleges have been heavily staffed with men originally trained to be ministers whose sensitivity to social ills and whose troubled consciences led them to look for a more realistic answer than could be found in the theological training of their period.

Among the great leaders of this movement were Walter Rauschenbusch, Francis Peabody, Washington Gladden, and Graham Taylor. These men and innumerable others were eagerly desirous that there be a widespread knowledge of the life of Jesus and of his idea of the Kingdom of God. Subsequently it has become apparent that the source of the evils of an undisciplined and unregulated economic life are unlikely to yield merely to a knowledge of Jesus' teachings. They are rooted in man's own stubbornness and pride and self-esteem. Religious-minded people were unprepared to recognize these manifestations of self-centeredness in an industrial era as a part of man's sinfulness. Also, account must be taken of the fact that in a period when everything seemed to be getting better and better the idea of sin could hardly expect to enjoy popularity. A God who judges does not meet eager acceptance. Today at least there are many who acknowledge that self-righteousness, in the economic order as in anything else, is one form of man's sinfulness, and there is no escaping judgment upon us for it.

WHAT DOES THE CHRISTIAN FAITH CONTRIBUTE TO PRESENT-DAY DECISIONS?

The preceding section is a greatly condensed review of the concern of the church and the Christian faith for economic life. As "new occasions teach new duties," so the Christian faith and its institutions are tested under new conditions. We have not passed this way before. Man, in his essential nature, remains the same. Society as the association of men remains the same, though under sharply different circumstances from those that prevailed in primitive or agrarian societies.

There is nothing about industrial society that changes the fundamental nature of man's relationship to his Creator and to his fellow men. He is still a creature of God and a brother to his fellow men, as a child of a common Father. Despite the fact that man is seemingly less dependent upon his fellow men because his dependence is less evident, he is actually, perhaps, even more dependent. Let the central electric-power-producing station fail to perform and what happens to man's independence? The resources of science and technology have created an illusion of independence both from God as Creator and from man as his co-worker and brother.

But events of recent months have served to jar our complacency. We have been stunned with the fact that in the hands of a comparatively few men lie the possibilities for life or death. Disclosure of the hitherto unknown structure of the atom has revealed to man in a new form the orderliness of nature's structure and the consequences if this knowledge is abused.

Between World Wars I and II, with a world-wide economic collapse in the wake of America's economic difficulties, a marked change in our understanding of the relationship between religious values and economics began to take place. There were still many in the United States who felt that what was needed was a larger measure of socialization of the economy. But increasing familiarity with the Russian experiment and its consequences cast grave doubts on such hopes or convictions. Then the necessity of putting the Western economy on a war basis temporarily called attention away from the fundamental problems and created an artificial prosperity. But the problem was still there.

Simultaneous with the fading of the depression, the rise of Hitlerism, and the expansion of Russian communism, there was held, in 1937, the Oxford conference on the "Life and Work of the Church." The date, 1937, is of great significance, for it marks the coming to maturity of the religious-ethical-social thinking of a great body of Protestantism. It is also of significance that those fostering another main line of religious thinking, the "Faith and Order" movement, which similarly had many years of preliminary exploratory background, held their conference at the same time and in the same country. From that date the "Christian Life and Work" and "Faith and Order" movements were merged in a single movement out of which developed the World Council of Churches, which held its first conference in Amsterdam in 1948.

The importance of these two main lines of thought combining and bringing their witness to bear upon the most critical issues of the modern age will hardly be lost on any discriminating reader. All this reveals the fact that leadership in the churches has been seeking to discover and make apparent to ever widening circles the profound truth of the gospel's relevance to all of life.

A summary of some of the points made in the reports of the several world and national conferences of Christian bodies will reveal something of the depth and scope of Christian thought in economic matters. The Oxford conference of 1937 related Jesus' commandment to the modern situation: the chief end of man is to love and glorify God, and this obligates man to love his neighbor as himself. This obligation arises not so much from man's inherent dignity as from the fact, revealed through Christ, that God loves men and wills to redeem them.[3]

Following World War II and the demise of Hitler there was held at Amsterdam the first session of the World Council of Churches. Section 3 of that session, called "The Church and the Disorder of Society," has been reported in the now celebrated *Man's Disorder and God's Design*, a book that the reader is urged to see. The Christian church, this book states, "approaches the disorder of society with faith in the Lordship of Jesus Christ." The present disorder may be attributed to two factors: one is the vast concentrations of power in the world— economic power under capitalism and economic and political power under communism. The other is the technology that dominates society and causes it to be controlled by the momentum established in earlier periods. But this control is not an inescapable necessity. No disorder in society can destroy the certainty that all men's lives belong to God and all men are duty-bound to seek God's Kingdom. It is the duty of the Christian church to help men achieve a full personal life in the modern technical society.[4]

The second World Council of Churches assembly, held at Evanston, Illinois, in 1954, included in its report deeply moving and far-reaching statements concerning the Christian's social responsibility. This responsibility is grounded in the mighty acts of God, who, through Christ, "has established with men a living relationship of promise and commandment in which they are called to live in faithful obedience to His purpose." All families, societies, and nations—all human groups—are responsible to God. The knowledge that we live in a "responsible society" provides us with a criterion for judging all existing social orders and a standard to guide us in our individual specific choices.[5]

Since its formation in 1908, the Federal Council of Churches has had departments or staff members especially responsible for interpreting this relationship between religion and economic life. In 1947 a conference was held in Pittsburgh under the auspices of the Federal Council of Churches. Its purpose was to foster "a continuing and comprehensive study of the relationship of Christianity to the economic order." This was followed in 1950 by another conference in Detroit on the theme "The Responsibility of Christians in an Interdependent Economic World." The report of that conference asserts that, since the Gospel is concerned with all the activities of man, "the Christian faith is relevant to the economic order." No one economic order can be identified with the Gospel, but all economic systems should be judged by the imperatives of the Christian faith; the most important of these is that "Christians confronting economic issues first accept Jesus Christ as Lord." This means that Christians are bound by loyalty to Christ and pledged "to make His Way regnant in the economic life." In considering any economic proposal they ask not whether it is communistic, socialistic, or capitalistic but only whether it is Christian.[6]

Then, in Pittsburgh in 1956 was held the third in the historic series under the auspices of the Department of Church and Economic Life of the National Council of Churches in the U.S.A. This time the theme was "The Christian Conscience and an Economy of Abundance."

The prophetic conference message directs attention to
the fact that we have entered a new era in which we can
produce more than at least some of the people need. But
man serves only as a trustee of the resources God has provided. The needy of the world are his brethren. We are
not prepared for the role which prosperity thrusts upon us
and we are in danger of being corrupted by it. The Christian conscience needs refinement and discipline under
these new circumstances and it cannot be at ease until
exploitations, lack of educational opportunity, and racial
barriers are eliminated.

An obvious common thread runs through all the summarizing statements of the leadership in these major
church conferences. There is an acknowledgment of God's
sovereignty for the whole of man's life. For many men, as
they have sensed their relationship to God, there has
emerged a growing understanding of the way in which
God has revealed himself to men in the person of Jesus
Christ. This is what is meant by the assertion that we find
the meaning for ourselves in life as it becomes clarified
for us in the significance of Christ as interpreter and re-
vealer of God's will and way. Christ as the symbol of
God's love establishes the ultimate pattern of human conduct and aspiration. In Him the meaning of the term
"neighbor" takes on new significance.

APPLICATION OF ETHICAL
PRINCIPLES IN THE
ECONOMIC ORDER

At the Detroit Conference on the Church and Economic Life, there was a resounding unanimity in support
of the general Christian *principles* as they apply to social
and economic life. When, however, the discussion turned
to the *specific application* of these principles, the unanimity disappeared.

For a number of years the Department of Church and Economic Life of the National Council of Churches has been attempting to hammer out and refine a statement that would be, as nearly as possible, definitive for, and universally acceptable to, Protestant groups. Such a statement has been completed and has been accepted almost unanimously by the general board of the National Council of Churches. The main points of this statement may be summarized as follows:

(1) Efficiency must be given a high priority in any appraisal of economic practices. (2) Christians will seek at least a minimum standard of living for all. (3) Economic institutions shall be judged by their consequences to family life. (4) All forms of discrimination shall be opposed. (5) Honest work shall be the obligation (and opportunity) of every worker. (6) Motives for security and advancement must be weighed against social responsibility and a sense of Christian vocation. (7) Fuller opportunities for private ownership and individual decision should be fostered. (8) A large measure of inequality destroys fellowship, though great danger is involved in attempting to coerce equality. (9) Christians are under the obligation to participate in political action since in it decisions affecting economic life are made. (10) Economc decisions in America inevitably affect the world situation. The principle of stewardship is therefore involved in making them. Finally (11) Christians must understand movements of social protest, especially those that seek to eliminate injustices perpetuated by existing arrangements.[7]

NECESSITY FOR A NEW APPROACH

It has become increasingly popular to use the threat of Russian supremacy as a device to get Christians to conduct themselves in economic life as Christians should.

There can be hardly any doubt that the rapid strides Russian communism has made constitute a threat for all freedom-loving nations and peoples. But to coerce Christians to act responsibly simply because Russia will win if we fail to do so is a questionable device. The simple fact is that we must conduct ourselves as Christians in economic life even if there be no communist threat. Communism is unacceptable for the same reason that other secular interpretations and demonstrations are offensive. Communism may be more vicious in its application, but the principle behind it is the same as the one that characterizes some of the economic activity under our present form of capitalism.

Christians have been lulled into false competition and doubtful security because of the way in which Christianity has been identified with economic life as we have come to know it, particularly economic life in the United States. About this issue much clarification is needed.

The forms of expression of our present economy may not be as brutal as the forms of expression and the concentrations of power in Russian communism. This tempering may be the product of a whole series of Christian influences in our culture. But these do not keep the secular purposes of our culture from being any different in their root form from the purposes of the economics of communism itself. W. G. Peck has pointed out this similarity in the secular emphasis of communism and much of the economy of Western nations: "The very shape and size of our cities, the shrunken condition and false assumptions of agriculture, our swollen industrialism," and all our education and culture reflect the secularism of our way of life. Our lives are overshadowed by the possibility, if not the probability, of the next world war occurring at no remote date. All this has uprooted men and women from the Western tradition and directed "their attention to the panorama of vulgarity perpetually presented to them." As a result, they not only have forgotten piety, they "have become largely incapable of understanding the traditional terms in which the Christian religion speaks."[8]

Should the communist threat subside, the problem with which we are here concerned would still be with us, namely, the spiritual nature of any enduring economic order.

It is possibly too much to expect that a great number of persons will increasingly comprehend the manner in which our economic order has developed since the modern period began and the relationship of religious life to it. There is a substantial number who already recognize the nature of the problem brought to us with the coming of the industrial era. Some persons want to return to the life of the Middle Ages with its completely stratified and well-ordered existence. Such nostalgia is devoid of any sense of realism; such an accomplishment could be purchased only at the price of the freedoms we have come to take for granted. It seems an inescapable fact that whatever success we attain must be achieved within the technical, scientific, and industrial order which has been brought to pass through man's achievements in science and technology. The question seems to be whether we can appraise these gains in their proper perspective and hold all things subordinate to an order of life which is itself subject to God's judgment. This involves a maturing on the part of religious people. Our chance for achieving harmony and decency in the world economy will be in direct proportion to the religious maturity of American leadership.

CHAPTER III

LABOR AND INDUSTRIAL RELATIONS

When the American Federation of Labor and the Congress of Industrial Organizations merged in 1955 to form the AFL-CIO, there was both rejoicing and shuddering. The rejoicing was on the part of those who hoped for a united labor movement in America. The advocates of such uniting forces believed that only thus could labor possess the strength it needed to accomplish its chosen ends. The shuddering—if that is not too strong a word—was on the part of those who look with misgiving upon the formation of another vast center of power. They feared what such a concentration of power might do to the rest of the nation, politically and economically.

Americans in general and Protestants in particular have entertained varying attitudes toward the labor movement. In a large measure those attitudes have tended to be unfriendly. This is not difficult to understand. Protestant churches are heavily influenced by the agrarian tradition in American life and by a suburban middle-class membership that is likely to sympathize with management. They have never felt at ease with the labor movement, reflecting as it does the growing industrialization of America. Our roots until recently have been predominantly rural. A strong emphasis upon personal piety and individual righteousness in rural life has made it difficult for Americans to accept easily the fact that decisions affecting the lives of many people are made not by individuals but by powerful groups and organizations. We were accustomed to assume that good men make good decisions. Then came the labor movement and its leadership which challenged some of these so-called good decisions. The workers refused to accept wage rates and working conditions dictated by business managers. They even questioned some of the economic principles of those managers. To such heresies was added the fact that many labor leaders had foreign origins and the people they led did not attend English-speaking churches.

Few church people identified the problem as one of *power* and *responsibility*, yet basically this was what it was—and is. It remains the key issue in political and economic life. Religious-minded people in general and Christians in particular sense that the exercise of power is a moral concern. Decisions affecting the lives and experiences of people are consciously or unconsciously based on our beliefs about the nature of man and society. And, as we have been trying to say, such beliefs are fundamentally theological.

The basis for the church's relation to the problem of power and its use in industrial society has never been very clear, for the very reason that the church has not grappled with this issue extensively in modern society. This is understandable in view of the comparative newness of the industrial era. It is not to be wondered at, therefore, that some of the attempts have been inadequate. But at least not all churchmen have been sitting on the side lines twiddling their thumbs or washing their hands of the whole complicated business.

Perhaps Protestantism's most unique and effective contribution to religious thought in America has been the Social Gospel. The type of religious emphasis characterized by that title represented an attempt in this country to cope with the evils of power concentration. The leaders of the movement realized that a process was going on which needed the ethical guidance of Christian standards. This meant subordinating personal gain to the social good. It meant developing counterforces to restrain those whose consciences were untouched by what Christ would seemingly require of men. It meant a genuine concern for working people, hence the vigorous support to the labor movement. Though the Social Gospel reflected a much-needed emphasis in Christian thinking, we now, from a somewhat more ample perspective, can recognize that it was possibly using inadequate weapons and a faith of insufficient depth.

With the rise of large combinations in industry as well as of a united labor movement, it has become apparent that individual action, however righteous, will not suffice to meet abuses of power. Only what has been called "a countervailing power" can be expected to provide a balance and an approximate justice.

John K. Galbraith contends that "the operation of countervailing power is to be seen with the greatest clarity in the labor market where it is also most fully developed. . . . The economic power the worker faced in the sale of his labor—the competition of many sellers with few buyers—made it necessary that he organize for his own protection."[1] Gradually it has become apparent to thoughtful Christians that, if workers are to be even moderately effective in a complex society, they require a force capable of matching corresponding concentrations of power in management.

PURPOSES OF THE LABOR
MOVEMENT

The labor movement, in addition to whatever benefits it may bring to its members by way of security, fellowship, and dignity, serves as a check on those whose decisions affect the lives of industrial workers. But who, one may ask, serves as a check on the decisions of labor? The conditions of employment established by management are obviously a primary check. Also, theoretically and, in most cases, actually, democratic processes in union organization

provide a measure of guaranty that those exercising decisions are acting in representative fashion.

But of increasing importance in the decisions of both
labor and management is sensitivity to the public good.
It is here that the influence of the church and its concern
for individuals and society has special relevance.

OPINIONS OF CHURCH PEOPLE

Because so much emotion has been generated by the
subject of labor organizations, it is sometimes difficult for
Christians to see the issue in its larger perspective. But
the church is not pro-labor or pro-management. If it is to
fulfil one of its functions in contemporary society, however, it must be pro-justice. Church people, just like any
others, are tempted to take sides quite independently of
any factors of justice. However fair and righteous we may
desire to be, there are influences that outwit us. There are
some who, out of a deep loyalty to the labor movement,
have sought to identify the church and that movement.
There are others, formerly a substantially greater number,
who have felt that the church must stand on the side of
the employer and management. In both instances, where
the loyalty is on a class or group basis, the Christian emphasis is betrayed.

This is, however, not the same as saying that the church
as a fellowship of Christians never takes a stand upon
issues involving labor or management. When Christians,
individually and collectively as a fellowship, work to en-
hance the dignity of man or challenge a monopoly, they
are not giving blanket indorsement to labor as such. They
are working for what they believe to be God's will for his
children. Similarly, when church people side with representatives of management to break the strangle hold of
monopoly or dishonest administration in a labor union,
they are not by this act primarily indorsing management.

52

They are struggling to achieve a workable harmony in society to save labor from its inner foes.

Many of the strains and tensions within churches stem from the struggles to understand the relationship between the Christian faith with its doctrine of man and the economic order which has so recently come into being. However, substantial resources are now available to people who prefer to base their decisions upon evidence rather than upon mere prejudice. Social psychology has made us much more understanding of the forces which determine our thinking. We know that the kind of work in which we are engaged and the social setting in which we live has much to do with the way we think and act. Even our religion, which supposedly gives us the values and ideals for guiding the rest of life, is itself often influenced by these same forces. Christians need continually to increase their awareness of obstacles which prohibit them from relating their religious life realistically to one of today's major issues.

The composition of certain of our larger denominations reveals how the attitudes of Protestant church people are influenced by their work and by where they live. The proportions of manual laborers and white-collar workers in the church membership have presumably had much to do with the attitudes of churches and church people toward labor. One study indicates that approximately 19 per cent of the total church membership belongs to trade unions (see table on p. 54).

Note that in many of the denominations the number of church members belonging to trade unions is less than the number in either the "white collar" or the "farmers" category. Also note that in certain denominations—Congregational, Episcopal, Presbyterian, and Methodist—the trade-union members are heavily outnumbered by those in business and professional activities. Add to these statistics the fact that the policies of many of the denominations are determined by representatives of the wealthier churches located in the suburbs and not by representatives of urban churches where the labor membership is greater. It is not surprising, then, that the Protestant church membership is but slightly informed as to the purposes and aspirations of labor.

OCCUPATIONAL CATEGORIES AND TRADE UNION MEMBERSHIP
IN MAJOR RELIGIOUS BODIES, 1945–46*

RELIGIOUS BODIES	PERCENTAGES BY OCCUPATIONAL CATEGORIES				PERCENTAGE BELONGING TO TRADE UNIONS
	Business and Professional	White-Collar Workers	Urban Manual Workers	Farmers	
Entire sample...	19	20	44	17	19
Catholic........	14	23	55	8	28
Jewish..........	36	37	27	0.6	23
Methodist.......	19	19	39	23	14
Baptist.........	12	14	52	22	16
Presbyterian.....	31	21	31	17	13
Lutheran........	13	18	43	26	20
Episcopalian.....	32	25	36	7	13
Congregational..	33	19	28	20	12

* Liston Pope, "Religion and the Class Structure," *Annals of the American Academy of Political and Social Science*, March, 1948, p. 87.

LABOR MEMBERSHIP IN THE CHURCH

It is noteworthy, however, that the proportion of top labor leaders affiliated with churches is greater than the proportion in the population of the nation. This may come as a surprise to many people. A survey of two hundred top AFL and CIO leaders reveals that approximately 90 per cent of them belong to a church or a synagogue. The membership affiliation follows:[2]

Protestant .... 51 per cent
Roman Catholic .... 35 per cent
Jewish .... 4 per cent
No affiliation .... 10 per cent

No canvass has ever been made of the total working population, particularly industrial workers, to ascertain the percentage of church affiliation. However, one does not need statistics to prove that urban manual workers generally do not constitute a vigorous and powerful segment of the church population. Those who have lived in urban industrial communities know that the church is not very important in the life of many industrial workers.

One of the most delicate and at the same time most tragic aspects of modern religious life is the absence of industrial workers from active participation in the life of the church. In Europe many Laymen's Institutes have come into being since World War II for the purpose of interpreting the significance of the Christian faith to those who have left the active life of the church or who have never known this relationship. Some similar ventures have been undertaken in the United States, but the results are as yet too insignificant to be credited with representing a trend. Even though labor leadership may be church-related in some measure, it is a common scandal in the Christian household that the middle-class religious life of America is not the place in which the spiritual growth of the industrial worker is nurtured.

This is not to imply that churches and religious nourishment are not available in industrial communities. Actually in those areas to which have come transplanted rural people from the South—both white and non-white—there are abundant churches of the "Pentecostal" type. Their architecture varies from simple store fronts to ultra-modern buildings. Their type of service runs the gamut from the familiar sermon of the preacher who accompanied his flock northward to one composed of parts borrowed from highly liturgical denominations. But the other-worldliness of the emphasis or the attempt to cushion the new arrivals against the harshness of urban living hardly relates the Christian faith to industrial life. These churches serve a purpose in facilitating the transition. They may help ease the tensions. But as yet the leaders without formal theological seminary training seem to be no more successful in interpreting the relation of the Christian faith to industrial life than the "trained" clergy. Congregations at all points along the economic scale have not grasped the significance of religion for industrial life.

As the great frontier of the church a century ago was the expanding rural geographic frontier, today it lies in the interpretation of the Christian faith to industrial man. And how well the church people understand the functions that the labor movement can perform may help determine how effective the interpretation may be. This involves not merely the church's supporting the labor movement but also its providing constructive criticism.

Here then is one clue to the dilemma—the people who comprise some 80 per cent or more of our churches do not know what lies behind the struggle of the labor movement. Parenthetically it must be said, too, that many workers are also unaware of their own history and purposes as a group. Obviously, both in churches and in the labor movement education and communication are urgently needed.

This chapter and this book are directed primarily to people now in the churches; for them there follows a greatly abbreviated review of the history of labor's progress as a movement.

A BRIEF HISTORY OF THE
LABOR MOVEMENT

At the time of the American Revolution, the population of this country was approximately 95 per cent rural. Very shortly thereafter, the pattern of urbanization, later greatly accelerated, became apparent. As industry and manufacturing developed, so did great cities—cities whose people could no longer return to the land when business cycles brought depressions. Workers became increasingly dependent upon their employers and the production of the machines they served.

The first strike in American history took place just ten years after the signing of the Declaration of Independence, when printers in Philadelphia struck for a minimum wage of six dollars per week. The first genuine labor union—the Cordwainer's (or shoemaker's) Union—was formed in the same city in 1792.

Because some individuals will, for their own benefit, undercut the price or wage established by men and women whose welfare requires a fair minimum, there arose the practice known as the "closed shop." From the time of the first unions until this very hour, the subject of the closed shop has been one of great contention. The closed shop, or one of its variations, is an inseparable part of the whole process of collective bargaining. It is certain that not until organized labor is freed from the influence of those who would undermine the status and gains of labor will the labor movement be willing to relinquish its demand for this form of security.

As industrialization increased in many areas of the nation, it was realized that it was not enough for a single union to insist upon decent wages, hours, and working conditions. Unless all workers, dependent upon the decisions and often the whims of those who owned or managed the machine, would act collectively, the individual gains to the various unions might be lost. Thus came into being the labor *movement*.

During the period of industrial growth in the early 1800's, labor unions united to press for free education. They were also effective in eliminating many of the sweatshops and the child-labor practices. But it required another seventy-five years for them to gain enough strength to eliminate most of the industrial practices that exploited the health of the workers.

In time of industrial crisis and panic, labor unions as well as the livelihood of workers suffered. The recurrence of booms and panics and their consequences to members of labor unions aroused present-day labor leadership to its very great concern for the total economic life of the nation.

The Civil War gave added impetus to transportation and the industrialization of all parts of the nation. The growth of corporations whose operations covered many states, and sometimes spanned the nation, necessitated unions with comparable geographic spread and internal strength. A corporation operating in several states could simply close down its plant in one area where there was a strike unless all workers in that industry united to meet the interests and needs of their co-workers.

During the period of transition from an agricultural to an industrial nation, the laws and the courts reflected the psychology of the industrial owners. A nation so recently rural had not grasped the fact that a person whose sole source of livelihood was a particular machine had a right to that machine and to what it could produce, so long as he tended it faithfully and its product was needed. However, the management that owned that same machine was readily granted this right.

There were still a few who could escape through the action made famous by Horace Greeley, whose slogan, "Vote yourself a farm," continued to hold out hope of escape. But already the free and purchasable land was becoming scarce. Industrial workers were being frozen in their jobs. The only release from conditions dictated by management was what could be attained by joint action known as collective bargaining. Where this failed, the last resort was a strike. Today in a nation whose population is more than one hundred sixty-five million, less than twenty-five million are now on farms, and the numbers dependent on industry continue to increase.

Shortly after the Civil War an attempt was made to establish a nationwide labor organization which would include many unions. The Knights of Labor, as it was called, met a genuine demand for a time but attempted to fight too many ideological battles. In the 1886 Haymarket Riot in Chicago, labor's attempt to secure an eight-hour day suffered a severe setback. Because many of those involved in the Haymarket Riot were also fostering a shorter work day, the whole idea was branded as "radical."

In the latter part of the nineteenth century the American Federation of Labor developed. Its leadership had learned to concentrate on what is called "business unionism": wages, hours, and working conditions. On the strength of this emphasis and concentration the AFL has achieved its present power.

When the AFL, whose members were primarily skilled craftsmen in varied lines, could not meet the needs of the mass industries where long training and apprenticeship were not essential (such as the automobile, rubber, and packinghouse industries), a new organization of unions was formed by some of the AFL leaders. This became known as the Congress of Industrial Organizations. Numerically the two great labor organizations were approximately equal. It is significant that the CIO came into being during the depression of the 1930's and was specifically aided by the Wagner Act of 1935, which encouraged the formation of unions. World War II heightened the demand for union action and markedly increased union strength. By the end of the war, there were approximately seventeen million union members who paid dues.

The increased strength of labor at the end of World War II, aided substantially by the support of President Roosevelt, produced a wave of opposition to unions. This opposition was based upon a fear that labor's power would be excessive and injurious to management. The tenor of the times reduced the labor support in Congress and brought about the Labor-Management Relations Act of 1947, known as the Taft-Hartley Act. Management contended that the Taft-Hartley Act was designed to make labor more responsible. Labor insisted that it was designed to prohibit further growth of the labor movement. Among management leaders there was grave apprehension regarding the growing power of labor in the political and economic life of the nation. Among labor leaders there was a corresponding concern lest labor lose the gains only recently made. The merger of the two largest organizations of labor unions must, thus, be seen against the background of this psychological climate.

In recent years there has been a growing tendency among labor leaders to emphasize labor's relations to the total economy. Labor has insisted that the whole economy can be healthy only if a proper proportion of industry's profits is paid to the laborer. Only thus can he continue to buy the goods industry produces, both while he is an active worker and after he is no longer able to be fully employed. This is the meaning of the growing emphasis upon "fringe benefits," that is, health insurance, pensions, and wage payments during enforced lay-offs. In the major industrial areas of the nation it is these issues which constitute some of the foremost concerns.

FUNCTIONS OF THE LABOR MOVEMENT

Of greatest significance is the fact that trade unionism has come to be recognized for what it is—an indispensable element in an industrial age. In addition, it is recognized that the real organizer is not any one individual, but the industrial organization itself—the plant, the mine, the industry. Thus the union has performed a fundamental service to the workers. It has made the worker "a free citizen of industry," increased his participation and influence in civic affairs, and provided him with new opportunities for rising socially. For this reason unionism has helped to make democratic government a reality and has strengthened the workers' attachment to democracy.[3]

Every major denomination in the United States has indicated its belief in the values and purposes of the labor movement. Presbyterians, for example, have stated that the failure to understand the contribution of the labor movement has led to much misguided criticism. The labor movement is necessitated by the deep wants of human nature and the basic character of industrialized society. The Presbyterians list some of the ways in which the unions have met these needs of the worker: (1) they have given him a sense of belonging; (2) they have afforded him a constructive use for his resentment against injustice and his demand for fair play; (3) they have helped him achieve a higher standard of living and better working conditions; (4) at their best, they have given the worker a chance to participate in the democratic organization of the union and have thus served as an agent for democracy; and (5) they have made available for the community and the nation the intellectual and social resources latent in the workers.[4]

But the hour-by-hour, day-by-day decisions in industrial relations are not concerned with the philosophy of labor, or of management, or of the theory of wages in the economy. They deal with the very mundane subjects of rates, working conditions, upgrading, etc. These are the fundamental issues of collective bargaining.

The history of the labor movement is a history of the struggle for the right to engage in collective bargaining. Because this process is indispensable to the achievement of justice and to the whole democratic process, the church has given its support to the idea and practice.

COLLECTIVE BARGAINING AND
INDUSTRIAL PEACE

When the National Planning Association sought to discover what made for industrial peace, they found that when firms accepted the idea of collective bargaining and entered into it in good faith, industrial peace was almost an inevitable result.[5] In each of the various industries used as the basis for the study, however, an indispensable factor was the willingness of each party to the bargaining to accept the prerogatives of the other. Under the heading "A Positive Approach to Peace" the authors suggest "that an overwhelming majority of contracts between employers and unions are negotiated or renegotiated peacefully each year and without work stoppages. Strikes make better newspaper copy and livelier congressional hearings than peaceful settlements."[6]

Desiring that the best insights of technical experts and religiously sensitive leaders be brought to bear on the problems of industrial relations, representatives of Catholic, Jewish, and Protestant affiliations have prepared an extraordinary document designed to foster and encourage better human relations in industry. In one sense it is a manifesto of common religious concern for the achievement of a better industrial society. It represents a mature approach to the whole problem. It observes that the real progress that has been made in providing the worker with sufficient food, clothing, and housing should not obscure the task left to be done. The worker must be made to feel that he is more than an automaton or a cog in a machine. In addition, the factory should be considered a true community rather than a battleground. A union that does not

62

feel it is continually struggling for survival is likely to work with the employer rather than against him.[7]

The Department of Church and Economic Life of the National Council of Churches has long been concerned for the rights of workers. In expressing itself on the issue of collective bargaining, it states that in all transactions between labor and management, both sides are subject to certain basic requirements. These include (1) responsibility to the public interest; (2) willingness to refrain from violence; (3) recognition of the other side's right to exist as an organization; (4) good faith in all agreements; (5) observance of established procedures of bargaining; (6) abstention from pressures that would lead to violation of the terms of the contract; and (7) abstention from employer-union collusion in prices and trade practices.[8]

However, the church is not leaving the settlement of conflicts between labor and management entirely to the leaders of the two groups. The role of the church in resolving such tensions is an active one. Courses in theological seminaries, summer institutes for ministers, summer seminaries in industry, schools of church and economic life, and many other activities reflect the growing awareness on the part of religious leaders of the profound importance of this issue. But, as was indicated earlier, the primary purpose of these various courses, schools, and institutes is not to secure the indorsement of either labor or management. Their purpose is to enable ministers to understand the broad scope of the issues involved.

As important as the training sessions for the clergy is the series of conferences for laymen from both labor and management groups in which industrial life is viewed from the Christian perspective. On the national level the Pittsburgh conference of 1947 on "The Church and Economic Life," the Detroit conference on a similar subject in 1951, and the Pittsburgh conference of 1956 made possible the common consideration of the problems of industrial life and the role of the Christian in relation to them.

Differences and tensions were not erased simply because they were viewed in the light of the Christian imperative. Possession of or commitment to the Christian faith does not guarantee freedom from conflict or from differences of opinion. It does, however, confront him who possesses that faith with the necessity of trying to understand the concerns of his brother and neighbor.

The Christian worker, whether he works with his hands or his mind or both, whether he is a worker or a manager, recognizes first of all that his work is performed not only for his gain but also as a service to his neighbor. This is one of the meanings of the term "Christian love." Work that dedicates one's talent to God is called a "vocation." To the Christian, thus, his work and the decisions arising from it are performed and resolved in God's service.

Few men in our time understand the main issues and the relation of the Christian faith to them as well as William Temple. He points out that the government of the firm for which a man works affects him more directly than the government of his state. Economic liberty is certainly as important to him, then, as political liberty. It is not enough for businesses to consult workers about regulations affecting hours and conditions of work if this consultation is granted as a favor. A voice in the government of his business is the right of the worker.[9]

It is true that such high hopes for the labor movement have not always been supported by the conduct of labor itself. One can easily point to the prostitution of power and influence at the hands of selfish and narrow men. But "hardboiled foremen and superintendents are matched by two-fisted union bosses; industrial dictators are greeted by power-hungry and despotic labor chiefs." Management's refusal to recognize the rights of labor causes labor to retaliate with long, unworkable contracts. In attaining their status, unions have developed men with habits of aggression that cannot be readily unlearned.[10]

ABUSES OF POWER

No account of the labor movement would be accurate or complete without reference to the abuses of power within unions and in dealings between unions and employers. Racketeers have acquired control of some unions. Apparently few unions have been wholly free from either dictatorship or the large-scale appropriation of union funds. The temptation of power and self-aggrandizement is as real in a labor organization as in business—or even in the church. Actually the pattern followed in the early stages of union development is not unlike the development patterns of business, of the church, or of the army.

It was thought that the union, in order to deal with the monolithic structures of business, required power as great as management's. Union leadership became a highly specialized function, and so it became necessary for one man to continue in office for some time. Presidencies of unions frequently became lifetime jobs, and this permanence led to abuses. The rank and file of the unions, unaware of the issues confronting the union and insensitive to the implications of their actions for all society, contributed to union irresponsibility. So long as they received new benefits, they paid little attention to how their leaders won them. They have suffered for this indifference. The gross misuse of union welfare funds by dishonest union officials and the racketeering in such unions as those operating on the waterfronts or in some phases of building construction would not have occurred if democratic practices had been faithfully followed by the union.

Much could be written about the indifference of union members, yet it is a tribute to the integrity of many union executives that they have been given the members' trust. Accurate accounting and full responsibility was not demanded of union leaders. What legislation finally required of industry it is now requiring of labor organizations in order to protect union members against irresponsible leaders.

There are some heartening signs, both in the labor movement and in management, of new attitudes in our economy. They are the product of a new type of leadership, and it in turn is creating more of its own kind.

THE CHURCHES AND
INDUSTRIAL LIFE

The National Council of Churches, like its predecessor the Federal Council of Churches, has issued a message each Labor Day Sunday. These messages reflect the changing thought and attitude of sensitive Christians toward the labor movement. Before labor had achieved a recognized position in American society, the message championed its cause exclusively. Now, however, it reflects an awareness of of labor's responsibility to the rest of society. The 1953 message reviewed the progress achieved in the forty years since the Labor Day messages began. The workers' hours had been shortened, their real wages increased, their working conditions improved, and their economic well-being strengthened. More and more workers had exercised their freedom to organize and to choose representatives to negotiate with their employers. The Christian church had indorsed this freedom and welcomed the even greater opportunities that the future held for the workers. New responsibilities, however, accompanied this freedom and opportunity. Labor was morally obligated to join with management, farmers, consumers, and other groups to work for the common good of society.[11]

Significantly, the 1956 Labor Sunday message dealt

with the problems of income security and technological change. Automation and a new concept of management's responsibility for continuing employment have changed the complexion of the issues.

There is a great contrast between the formation of the Cordwainer's Union in 1792 and the merger of the AFL and CIO in 1955. Similarly, there is a great difference between the "public-be-damned" attitude of an early railroad operator and the ultrasensitivity to public opinion of great corporations today, with whole departments responsible for creating good will.

Mature and responsible persons have long recognized that labor and management are mutually dependent and responsible to the rest of society. In fact, one of the genuine apprehensions of our own time is the likelihood of collusion between labor and management and the possibility that the good of the rest of society will be overlooked. Fortunately, there are policy-makers in both labor and management who know that this can be one of the unfortunate and harmful results of the co-operative relationship between the titans. An increasing number of church people are also aware of the need for appraising all economic action against a standard of a just and orderly society.

Christians, thus, should insist that the total welfare of society be considered rather than a particular segment, whether labor or management or some other. Knowing full well that there are still sections of the country where co-operative activity and harmony are not achieved, the Christian must judge the movements of the smaller segments of society in terms of their worth and value for the whole.

The role of the church, then, in relation to laboring people is to insist on justice for all. Assured of economic justice, men are free to consider their own destiny and the well-being of their neighbors. As the closing paragraph of the 1953 Labor Sunday message states: "In working for civil rights, increased production, job opportunities, adequate wages, social responsibility, and a free world community, we are working for each other, for ourselves, and for God who seeks to realize His purpose of justice and freedom in the affairs of men."[12]

CHAPTER IV

AGRICULTURAL POLICY

Even city people are now aware that agricultural policy affects them as well as farmers. Twenty-two depressions in the last hundred years have been preceded by falling agricultural prices. A series of wars has brought the issue of agricultural policy into prominence. Except for the problem of segregation, no single domestic issue in America is so charged with political and economic dynamite.

The solution to the agricultural problem, however, is not primarily the responsibility of people in the rural areas. The decisions attempting to resolve the problem must be made by a nation almost 90 per cent urban or non-farm. The effects of these decisions on farm people hold the key to the well-being of the rest of the nation.

The urgent necessity for fundamental decisions confronts us for the following reasons:

1. Our American economy is constantly imperiled by the weakness and instability of agriculture. The expression "depressions are farm-fed and farm-led," while not wholly accurate, has a measure of truth in it.

2. Surpluses trouble our consciences while there is malnutrition in our own country and starvation elsewhere. The farmer's efficiency was encouraged by the research of both the federal government and private organizations. Now, with his surpluses, the farmer is penalized for doing what he was once urged to do.

3. In other nations where people are starving it is well known that we have large surpluses. But dumping the surpluses would wreck the economy of many other nations and perhaps create an abnormal dependence upon benefactions.

4. In this land of prosperity and efficiency, approximately 1,380,000 farms out of 5,000,000 produce less than sub-

sistence for their operators. These farms are in areas of dire poverty in our rich land. The plight of the low-income farmer and the million or more migrants who follow the crops is one of the sore spots in our national life.

5. Movement out of agriculture into other occupations has been going on steadily for two hundred years. It may well be that the people who ought to be moving out, however, lack the opportunity and the capacity to do so.

6. American agriculture has its roots in the concept of the "family farm." Our national legislation presupposes this pattern. But forces in modern American agriculture disavow this fundamental tenet about our agricultural society.

These are some of the issues with which America is confronted today. Pressures are being exerted in order to improve each of these areas. Decisions about them are being made either overtly or by default. The Christian church is inseparably involved in all these decisions because fundamentally they are spiritual decisions. Recognition of this fact may give us a much-needed perspective.

RELIGIOUS RESOURCES

In chapter i we expressed the conviction that all matters of policy are decided on the basis of one's presuppositions, one's philosophy or theology. Fundamental religious convictions may not solve the agricultural dilemma, but any genuine solution will have to agree with the deepest insights of our faith regarding man and his society. How technical decisions are made and the standards against which they are appraised are of concern to thoughtful Christians. The Christian's basis of appraisal lies in his understanding of the nature of life itself, of man's relationship to his fellow man and to the source of his own being. His economics are the tools by which he implements his deepest desires.

70

Much of our Bible comes out of and deals with rural experience. For this reason rural people have found it easier to understand many biblical illustrations than have urban residents. As was indicated in our chapter on economics, chapter ii, it is now necessary to adapt this rural-oriented religious tradition to urban and industrial life. Man's relationship to his fellow men and to God may not be markedly different in a rural setting, but it is significant for us that our faith originated and was first tested in rural circumstances. We are now attempting to relate that faith to a decreasingly rural society.

We start with the assumption, which no one has expressed more majestically or profoundly than the psalmist, that "the earth is the Lord's." This is a revolutionary assumption; it at once places man in a stewardship relation to all of life. He does not own outright; he is but a representative and a custodian of the life and property within which he finds himself. Another expression of the same idea relates man to the earth in an even more intimate fashion: "The earth is man's home." He lives in it, he is dependent upon it, he finds his sustenance of body and soul in his life within that home.

In each of these two statements there is presumed a giver of life, a central figure essential to the "home." Primary, therefore, is the assumption of God's supremacy and centrality. Jesus' use of the term "Father" symbolized this both for the individual and for the greater family of mankind. In Jesus himself there has come to be recognized the symbol of the way in which God as Father deals with his children—with self-giving love. An example of the way in which man should live among and deal with his fellow men is thus provided. All matters of policy in whatever area ultimately have to be tested against this final norm for personal and social conduct.

The Apostle Paul sensed this interdependence of man-

71

kind and the especial obligation it placed upon those who understood the meaning of God's revelation of himself in Jesus Christ. Paul recognized the solidarity of mankind and for it used the descriptive assertion, "We are parts of one another" (Eph. 4:25), as suggested in chapter i. Whatever destroys the sense of brotherhood and of being "parts of one another" is sinful. Agricultural policy, economics, and everything else in human society is to be judged by this fact.

CAUSES OF OUR PRESENT CONDITION

The sensational growth in technology and agriculture has occurred within the lifetime of many readers. Through the familiar charts showing the increase in the use of combines, field choppers, manure scoops, milking machines, self-feeding silos, commercial fertilizers, and all the rest, the public has come to realize that a revolution has taken place in agriculture. The speed with which these innovations have become accepted is largely responsible for the urgency underlying our present need for an over-all agricultural policy.

Too, the declining need for agricultural workers constitutes a fact we have come to take for granted in our industrial society. Whereas in 1800 each agricultural worker supported four persons, he now supports almost eighteen. In contrast, a far greater percentage of people need to be involved in agricultural production in other countries. In China and India almost everyone labors at least part of the time to help produce food, and yet there is often famine. In Italy more than half the people work on the land, yet there is seldom an abundance of food. Great Britain for 150 years has imported the bulk of its food in exchange for industrial exports. Only about 7 per cent of her population is engaged in agricultural production, and not enough food is produced within the country to satisfy

the demand for it. In the United States less than 20 per
cent of the population lives on farms and only 15 per cent
of the labor force is engaged in agricultural production.
Yet there has never been a famine here. The population
has enjoyed the greatest variety and abundance of food of
any nation in the world's history.[1]

War, however, has contributed as much as any other
factor to the surpluses of agricultural products in America.
During both world wars farmers were asked to produce
more than they had ever produced before. Technical resources that otherwise might have taken many years to
be adopted were quickly put into operation. Lands that
otherwise would never have been plowed up were used as
a source of food. Wheat production, for example, was
increased during the war and postwar periods in response
to official action and contributed to our war effort and to
the recovery of Western nations after the war. After this
great volume was no longer needed, however, legislation
providing for adjustment was not put into effect.[2]

The present dilemma, thus, is not the product of greed
or overambitiousness on the part of farmers. It is the
result of a policy deemed essential for the winning of war.
Correspondingly, then, the solution of the problem is just
as much an obligation of the total nation as is the necessity for disposing of industrial plants and reducing war
production in industry. This fact is often forgotten when
the charges are made that the farmer is receiving too heavy
a benefit from the rest of the tax-paying public.

But there is excellent reason to believe that our "surplus"
created out of war pressures may not be due wholly to
overproduction. There is extensive evidence of dislocations
in other phases of our economy—of disparities in abilities
to consume. Rainer Schickele has suggested that "farm
surpluses except for a few special commodities during certain periods are the result of demand rather than supply

maladjustment, of under-consumption rather than over-production, and hence should be taxed primarily from the demand side."[3] Farm organizations and agricultural conferences attach varying degrees of importance to the inability of a large percentage of American people to purchase the kinds of food necessary for their physical well-being.

We are suggesting here, therefore, that one of the causes of the surplus is the fact that not everyone here in our own country enjoys a balanced diet and good physical health. The problem of low-income people in agriculture constitutes more than a problem of small farms and inadequate units of production. The low incomes in agriculture have only served to perpetuate the low incomes throughout the nation.

Finally, whereas in previous years approximately 10 per cent of our agricultural production went to other nations, this is no longer possible. Many nations to which we formerly shipped agricultural products are producing more adequately themselves; some of them are actually in competition with us. Either new markets must be found for that 10 per cent or we must curtail production proportionately. There are still, of course, many areas of the world in dire hunger. The problem is that of serving them in a way designed both to meet their immediate needs and to foster a stable economic and political life for them.

"FAITH, HOPE, AND PARITY"

Perhaps the best-known attempt to give the agricultural producer a measure of equality in the total national economy has been that of price supports based on "parity." Parity is a device, included in the Agricultural Adjustment Act of 1933, designed to give "prices to farmers at a level that will give agricultural commodities a purchasing power with respect to articles the farmers buy equivalent to the purchasing power of agricultural commodities in the base period." One of the continuing difficulties in the use of this formula has been the "base period." Originally, the years 1910–14 were used, since they, presumably, were years of normalcy. Subsequently, revisions in this formula have been made. "The 1948 revision specified that the relative parity prices were to be based on actual relative market prices for the ten preceding years. Thus farm products whose market prices were lagging behind the general level of farm prices would have their parity prices lowered."[4]

There is something seemingly fair about any attempt to give to the farmer for the products of his seed, feed, and fertilizer prices reasonably comparable to those he pays for feed, seed, and fertilizer. Unfortunately, parity prices have not been a uniform blessing. Since the government entered into agreements to purchase products at a percentage of parity (ranging from 90 to 60), many producers have found it more satisfactory to sell their products to the government. Though this has bolstered the income of a substantial number of farmers, it has also contributed to the problem of surpluses. The most notorious failure in this process was the supporting of potato prices, which in the end cost the federal government well over $584 million.

SURPLUSES AND PRICE SUPPORTS

Most references to price supports and government surpluses accumulated under them include the comment that the federal government now holds well over seven billion dollars worth of farm products. Not all this is lost, of course. In the event of a widespread drought or war most, if not all, of the surpluses would be utilized. Even without a major catastrophe a substantial portion of those surplus products will find their way into the streams of normal use. What is rarely reckoned in the public deliberations on this problem is the fact that "the total realized loss on all farm support programs from their inception through fiscal 1955 was two and one-third billion dollars. This cost incurred over a period of about twenty-two years has averaged somewhat above one hundred million dollars a year or less than a dollar a year for every person in the United States (based on average population over those years)."[5] The cost of all the price-support programs, including administrative costs, Commodity Credit Corporation losses, expenditures for surplus-removal purchases, and expenditures for export programs, aggregated $3.8 billion from 1933 to June, 1953. This amount is small compared to the total value of crops and livestock marketed during this period, which amounted to $335 billion.[6]

It should also be remembered that when industry ceases to function through curtailment of production the cost is largely borne by the taxpayer in the form of unemployment compensation and relief costs. Industry's discarded employees become dependent upon taxes. The farmer cannot cease to produce in the manner of the factory operator. His "plant" must continue to operate. In addition, industry has many price-support devices not at present available to the farmer. Many of them have been worked out in conjunction with the government. They include tariff and import quotas, retail price maintenance laws, regulations prohibiting unfair competition, and minimum wage laws. These public price policies are not so noticeable to the taxpayer because they do not involve significant appropriations from Congress.[7]

It would be impossible, of course, to estimate to what extent price supports based upon the parity formula or any other have served to save us from a major depression comparable to the economic catastrophes which occurred before the price-support program was part of national policy.

But price supports, though they are the most evident and most discussed of the programs designed to help solve the problem, are not the only attempts. Four others also of far-reaching implication may be mentioned. The first, crop production control, operates in conjunction with price supports. Producers who are granted price supports are expected to co-operate in a production program designed to limit the amount placed upon the market. Hence the support price has been tied to acceptance by the farmer of some kind of controls in acreage. These have not been wholly satisfactory. In many instances the value of a piece of farm land has been determined by the nature of the allotment given to it, particularly in tobacco farms.

Second, a commodity loan and storage program became a necessary sequel to the government's purchase of farm production. The steel bins that dot the countryside are symbols of this phase of the experiment. In World War II and the Korean War the storage of surplus grains in these structures provided a much-needed resource for security purposes. At the present time our total surplus in storage amounts to about 20 per cent of a single year's production. The difficulty, of course, lies in the fact that most of this surplus is wheat. No satisfactory formula has yet been worked out to provide protection against drought and an adequate reserve for defense.

Third, soil conservation was necessitated by our need for food for wartime purposes. The high productivity of our agriculture was bought at a very high price. Land which should have been left for grazing was turned into crop land. Crops such as cotton have been planted on the same soil year after year, regardless of the harmful effect to the productivity of the land. But the farmer's practices affect more than his own land. If he induces sheet and gully erosion, other farms bear the burden of the soil wash, and distant streams and harbors are filled up. Plainly, a farmer who lowers his own production costs by not practicing soil conservation is not held accountable for all the costs actually incurred in the production of his crops.[8] The development of conservation districts throughout the nation under the Soil Conservation Service, therefore, was necessary for preserving soil that was being lost to neighboring farms and to posterity.

Fourth, closely allied with the soil conservation program is the payment to producers for following specified procedures in the cultivation of their land. This is designed to preserve soil and assure high productivity for the future. Payments reward those who comply with crop reductions and those who shift to other crops. Unfortunately, most of the benefits of this program have gone to those who have least need of them. It has been practically without benefit to the very small producers with the lowest incomes.

SUGGESTIONS FOR AN AGRICULTURAL POLICY

It is significant that none of the major proposals for resolving the agricultural dilemma would have agriculture go back to a completely competitive situation in which prices would be determined by the open market. Obviously, if we are going to have a strong agricultural economy there will have to be some arrangement acceptable to both farmers and non-farmers. Industry is able to protect itself against falling prices by withdrawing its products from the market. In the depression of the thirties agricultural prices dropped 56 per cent but effected only a 6 per cent drop in production. At the same time the price of non-farm goods declined only one-half as much as farm goods. The farming industry involves such high risks and low returns that it would be unreasonable and unwise not to safeguard the farmer against the threat of general depressions.[9]

What, then, would constitute the basis for a desirable policy? Rainer Schickele lists the most valid criteria known to the author. A desirable policy would (1) gradually increase national income and improve the allocation and use of resources; (2) reduce the number of families living below subsistence by expanding the individual's opportunity to increase the rewards of his labor; (3) promote the stability of the general economy; (4) confer no special benefits without receiving from the beneficiary something of commercial value in return; (5) avoid excessive red tape and the restriction of constructive or harmless individual activities; and (6) avoid weakening individual initiative or causing undue reliance on public aid, either for business profits or for family living.[10]

Almost all the proposals, whether for high and rigid or low and flexible supports, take account of the necessity for removing from the farms a large number of individuals who cannot now make an adequate living in agriculture and whose farm operations are too small to assure any sizable commercial production. In ten southern states alone there are 2,625,051 low-income farms. In 1951 the top family money income in this group was $1,958 and the average approximately $1,689. In these southern areas off-farm income has not been as readily available as in the North, especially for non-whites.[11] Any sound agricultural policy must therefore provide for movement of many of these farm people into more productive activity and the consolidation of their non-efficient farms into larger producing units.

The suggestion that "efficient producing units" must be created raises one of the most fundamental problems in American agriculture, namely, the role of the family farm. Our national program for agriculture has been based on the family farm from its inception. The Pre-emption Act of 1841, the Homestead Act of 1862, the acreage limitation provisions of the Reclamation Act of 1902, and the Bankhead-Jones Tenant Purchase Act of 1937 have all based our national agricultural program on the family farm. There may be danger of sentimentality when the theme of the family farm is discussed. It has become one of the sacred flags. Actually, the family farm does not need mere sentiment for its support. It has been shown to be not only an efficient producing unit but also a source of the kind of life Americans have come to believe is basic to the well-being of the nation as a whole. A study of the contrasts in community and family life between two communities of markedly different farm types indicates, within the evidence available, that the family farm type is more likely to preserve the qualities we most desire in American life.[12]

Obviously, modifications in the description of the family farm become necessary with changes in technology, communications, etc. What was an adequate farm acreage a generation ago may be too small with today's machinery. Generally speaking, the family farm is one that is operated primarily by a single family, with occasional additional work performed either in exchange with others or by employed assistance. There are forces in American agriculture that tend to reduce the number of family farms and to change the quality of the life on them. The rise of corporation farms and multiple-chain-farming operations are a constant threat. Suffice it to say that no solid agricultural policy can be created which does not take account of our historic concern for the family farm.

The nation is constantly being pressed to decide whether it desires to foster this institution assumed to be a cornerstone in our agricultural economy. The issue of limitations on benefits to be paid to large-scale producers, for instance, is involved here. Most dramatic at this point are the price-support checks of more than a million dollars being paid to some farm operators. To date it has not been found possible or, apparently, desirable to limit the amount of government benefits accruing to large-scale producers. When

Charles Brannan was Secretary of Agriculture a limitation on support payments was proposed for the agriculture bill but it had to be deleted. In each succeeding proposed bill a similar stipulation has been suggested and then removed. It can be expected, however, that more of such legislation will be proposed.

Land retirement or removal of land from active production will constitute an inevitable part of any long-range policy proposal. Whether known as a soil-bank plan or an acreage-reserve the principle is the same. Land used to grow food of which there is a surplus is taken out of production and put to grass. Every proposal for agriculture's welfare insists on something of this sort. This means that the farmers are not to abandon new technologies but to apply them to fewer acres of crops and to fewer feed units. They should cull out their poorest acres and divert them to uses requiring lower in-puts per acre, changing wheat fields to grass, corn to hay and forage, and cotton and tobacco to corn, hay, and forage.[13]

There seems to be practically unanimous agreement that the cost of any such program, that is, the payment to the farmer for land which he takes out of production, is a legitimate charge against the national government and hence against the taxpayer. The problem was created for the benefit of the nation. The penalty should not be borne by individual farmers.[14] There is also no serious disagreement about the need to tie price supports to some plan for lowering the quantity of agricultural production.

But one all-too-obvious fact is that though land is taken out of production it is possible with intensive fertilizing to produce almost as much on a smaller acreage. Likewise, it has been possible to shift to the raising of other products which are already in oversupply, as, for example, the shift from cotton to corn. It would almost seem that this is a merry-go-round and that there is no answer.

There are, however, two main problems. One pertains to the using-up of surplus already in hand and the other to the forestalling of surpluses in the future. The solution to these problems is, as we have been suggesting, both to reduce the amount of acreage now in production and to increase the consumption of those now in need. Leonard Schoff points out that there are more than eleven million individuals in this country "dependent on federal and state allowances for their support. If these persons were consuming food at the average per capita they would be buying with their families enough to consume 5% more than is now consumed in the nation or one-half of all the present surplus. During the depression the food stamp plan enabled a large part of the American people to have a decent diet and by that plan the economy itself was immeasurably bolstered."[15]

The upper four-fifths of our population would probably spend little more for food if their incomes were increased. The lowest fifth would presumably use most of their increase for food. In this lowest fifth are the people living on pensions and aid programs.

At still longer range, but inseparable from the total problem, is the educational level of the millions now on small, unproductive farm units and earning the lowest incomes in the nation. Consumption patterns are closely correlated with education. A national program for increasing the educational level will have a profound effect upon agricultural consumption and is, therefore, an inseparable part of our agricultural policy.

No consideration of agricultural well-being in this country would be complete without making provision for the low-income worker in agriculture. There are about a million migrant workers following the crops and another million with more permanent employment who are also underpaid. Certainly one of the greatest tragedies in our

American economy is the deterioration of life that accompanies migrant life. Such studies as that of the President's Commission on Migratory Labor (1951) and Shirley E. Greene's *The Education of Migrant Children* (1954) constitute one of the most damaging indictments of what has appeared up to now to be our incapacity to remedy one of the sore spots in our national life. This deserves much more comprehensive treatment than can be given here.

Integral to the whole issue of agricultural policy, also, is the question of natural resources and their conservation. Stirred by the fear that our profligacy in the treatment of resources may impair our life as a nation and our future as a people, we have taken extraordinary steps already to assure continuance of productivity from the soil and from our other resources. The Soil Conservation Service, which almost blankets the nation with its districts providing technical counsel for all who will take advantage of it, constitutes one of the far-seeing measures to offset this potential calamity. Certain basic facts about the soil have percolated into our school curriculums: the amount of soil that has already gone down the rivers and is irreplaceable, the amount of good earth which is taken off with every large rain, etc. What has not been as fully interpreted is the fundamental religious significance of the conservation of resources. The fact that many agricultural programs are tied to soil conservation attests to our concern for the problem. The deeper meaning of man's relationship to the earth remains to be more comprehensively and impellingly told. The report of the third National Study Conference on the Church and Economic Life, which dealt with the theme "The Christian Conscience and an Economy of Abundance," recommended that the churches study conservation as a challenge to the Christian conscience. The selfishness and greed of generations before us and of our own generation have often led to the exploitation and waste of the earth's resources. Ignorance of conservation methods, indifference arising from seemingly inexhaustible supply, competition in free enterprise, and governmental corruption have also contributed to this waste. Christians should encourage discriminating and conscientious concern for natural resource conservation through the churches' devotional, educational, and social action programs.[16]

WHAT CAN THE CHRISTIAN DO?

Within recent months many public-minded and nonpartisan organizations have formulated policy statements dealing with agriculture. Their findings, though objective, do not necessarily provide a pattern wholly acceptable to the citizen who would arrive at public policy in the light of his Christian faith. Nevertheless, the Christian realizes that any solution must take into account the use of economic insights and practices. His task is to appraise the probable results in the light of their consequences to the whole of God's order.

In 1948 there was held, under the auspices of a number of interdenominational agencies, a conference to prepare a statement on a Protestant program for the family farm.[17] While many denominations had issued statements about problems in agricultural life,[18] it was not until 1951 that the first national conference on the churches and agricultural policy was held.[19]

The dates of these conferences are important. It has become increasingly apparent that the agricultural problem was only delayed with World War II and the Korean War. The studies we have discussed were made under various auspices but represent a mounting concern about this issue. Another book, *Social Responsibility in Farm Leadership* (1956), appeared still more recently, one of a series on ethics in economic life. It deals wholly with agricultural problems and the responsibility for helping to solve them.

Its author, Walter W. Wilcox, is an agricultural economist who has been a consultant to congressional agricultural committees and to the United Nations Food and Agriculture Organization. He confronts church people in particular with the full dimensions of the agricultural problem.

It is not yet apparent to any large Protestant group that religious life is closely identified with and may be strongly influenced by agricultural policy. Perhaps the pressure of events will force the individualistic church membership to be aware of the mutual dependence of all people—rural and urban.

As one of the reports states, the church, as a nationwide and worldwide fellowship, must sense the consequences for all people of any policy. Matters of agricultural policy "are inseparably related to the basic material resources of man's life and the physical and social conditions under which abundant life may be achieved."[20]

Not all church people can be expected to take interest in this concern, in spite of its universal importance. It is reasonable to expect, however, that, in areas depending for their livelihood on agricultural pursuits where church members are farmers, the churches will recognize the issue as an integral part of their religious life.

One of our difficulties heretofore has been the lack of available material on the religious significance of agricultural problems. Many church people are reasonably well informed about rural life in ancient Palestine. But they have not transferred their religious concern to rural life in the United States. The interest in the theological aspects of agricultural life may not yet have reached high tide, but it represents a heartening trend.

There is a wholesome awakening among farm, industrial, and labor leaders to the basic meaning and significance underlying all aspects of our economy. A wholesome maturing process is taking place among the thoughtful and responsible leaders in our national economic life. It may be too early to find such genuine searching throughout our churches, but it is apparent there is a stirring and a slowly rising concern.

For all Christians who have sensed that the frontiers of Christian life are in economics and especially, perhaps, in agricultural economics, there is an increasing abundance of informative and interpretative material. Working individually, through church groups, through farm organizations, and in many allied ways, the Christian can help effect a solution to the agricultural problem.

CHAPTER V

RACE

Any description of the current situation in race relations is out of date almost before the ink is dry. Nevertheless, the fundamental issues remain unchanged. Despite the *legal* aspects of segregation, the *social* and *psychological* explanations supporting gradualism, and the *economic* argument, the issue is primarily and essentially *religious*. But religion is not something apart from other phases of life. As we have stated frequently, everything pertaining to human well-being must ultimately be seen in relation to man's basic nature and his destiny as a human being. Our attempt to meet the issue of race on lesser grounds has created the tragic situation in which we as a nation and other nations as well are involved. No amount of self-righteousness, however skilfully phrased, will eliminate this fact. It is recognized, of course, by many Christians who, both in the South and in the North, are earnestly and prayerfully attempting to heal the wounds created by color segregation. The soul-wrenching issue does not yield merely to an ideal, however perfect. The informed Christian knows this; yet he can never forget that the solution he seeks must conform to what he honestly believes is God's will.

The realistic Christian also knows that the two-thirds of the world's population which is dark-skinned is greatly impressed by the arguments of Communist representatives that America in general and Christians in particular are hostile to their best interests. In the contest for men's loyalties we have carelessly handed the most powerful weapon of all to our major opponents. Over 500 million were attracted to the enemy camp and captured, in part at least, with weapons we thoughtlessly gave to our opponents. There seem to be many Americans who would rather lose to communism than conduct themselves as Christians in their relations with God's dark-skinned children.

The Christian should also know that visitors to America from lands populated by colored people have often been treated in a way that makes nations and people doubtful about America's integrity. Meanwhile, many of our own American citizens are so consumed with the wrongs done them that their latent capacities for constructive usefulness are sorely impaired—to say nothing of the tragic injury to their own inner lives. The presence of a determination on the part of some individuals to foster a superior-inferior status among American people serves as a depressant, a little-recognized and rarely discussed strangulation of the best in our national life. The presence of this blind spot in the religious life of individuals and groups undercuts our spiritual vitality and drags on the religious life of individuals, of churches, and of the nation.

The race question affects not only the inner life of the nation, however. A national crisis resulting from a Supreme Court decision based on the fundamental law of the land threatens open hostility. Physical violence over the right to decent living space and educational opportunity is warping lives and making warring camps of once-peaceful communities.

Though it is true that the race problem has been with us a long time, the acceleration of communications and travel gives it a terrifying urgency today. Already we have lost some major battles. Pride and prejudice, usually inseparable, have blinded us to the importance of the problem and the disastrous consequences already suffered. Christians will recognize that this is fundamentally a spiritual problem.

CHRISTIAN IMPERATIVES

We start with the assumption that as Christians we are a company of people intrusted with God's order. Whatever we do, therefore, must be viewed against the final command and standard for us—what does God's order require of us? We are obligated to help create a society as near as possible to what we believe God would have it be. It is possible that the present tragic situation has come about in part because individuals have sought to escape responsibility for the kind of society we have by insisting that God would create whatever kind of order he desired.

Gunnar Myrdal, in the most comprehensive study of race ever made in America, concludes that the problem has come to its present proportions because Americans, with their particular religious background, tend to profess one thing in their religious life and their political ideals and then to act in another way. The result is a guilty conscience that causes Americans in general and Christians in particular to avoid facing reality.[1]

Presumably, a Christian is one who eagerly seeks out the facts on any issue affecting human life. We are desirous of knowing why we act as we do and why others act as they do. Earnestly and honestly we seek the light of God's revelation and its meaning for all phases of human life. It may be the partial and selective appropriation of portions of the Gospel for our own use that has contributed to our sinfulness. We should, therefore, welcome every insight from the Bible, the record of God's relations with men.

But there are facts and pieces of wisdom which come to us from sources other than the Scriptures. Since all truth and the search for truth is a part of God's order, we avail ourselves of these added resources. We owe much to those who have pinpointed and clarified some of the basic reasons for our racial attitudes.

89

TENSION BETWEEN RACES

No single list could include all the reasons for differences of opinions and tensions between people of different races. There are some, however, which stand out prominently. First, a whole group of people, readily identified by color, have historically been in an inferior position. A necessity for feeling that some other group is inferior has been perpetuated, and no amount of proof to the contrary carries much weight. The American creed of the equality of all men is overlooked when there is the need to feel that others are inferior. We know enough about human behavior to know that people who must feel superior are frightened or warped or sick, or perhaps all three.

Second, either for protection or perhaps quite honestly, many have been under the illusion that colored people are intellectually inferior and incapable of participating in a culture of the quality that some white people have attained. By now this illusion has been completely dispelled. Few facts are more thoroughly documented than the equal learning ability of all races, given similar opportunity and conditions.

Third, consciously or unconsciously in the minds of many is the fear that their economic security is threatened by large numbers of skilled and unskilled workers in another race group. In fact, for many persons who have carefully analyzed it, the whole race question boils down to this problem of economic insecurity and the threat involved in the ascendancy of another race. This threat may have seemed more plausible a few generations ago than now. By now we know that increase in skill and competence adds more than itself to the total well-being. It stimulates an increasing quantity of like or additional skills and makes increased resources for all.

Fourth, the riots and open conflicts in American cities

where other groups have moved into predominantly white areas have often grown from a fear of property depreciation. It is now well known that much of this hysteria was fostered by those who stood to make substantial gains from forcing the sale of property. Areas available to Negroes were, for the most part, already approaching slum conditions. Conversion of single residences into multiple dwellings hastened deterioration and would have done so no matter who lived there. On the other hand, some of the best-kept-up single residences are those where Negroes have had the opportunity to express their pride in attractive surroundings.

Fifth, people are frightened because they think the proximity of whites and non-whites might encourage interracial marriages. The evidence does not bear this out. It is a curious paradox that what white people suspect the Negro desires greatly he actually desires least—intermarriage; whereas what the Negro really wants most the whites actually fear least—economic security.[2]

Sixth, the fear of being outnumbered and outpowered, politically and numerically, has contributed to the desperation of those who anticipate such difficulties. To reply that while this situation is being adjusted those who are being outnumbered will suffer what the more numerous colored people have known for generations is hardly an answer. Nevertheless, if justice is to be expressed and our democratic processes are to be trusted, this is a risk that will have to be taken. Any excessive use of power by those who have acquired it (in traditional American fashion) has been infinitesimal in contrast to the injustices wrought against the Negro people in this country.

Finally, there are biblical statements that seem to support racial segregation. Probably they are less a reason for discrimination than a rationalization used by those who want to discriminate because of their own pride or fear.

The fact is that there is no biblical scholar esteemed by his colleagues today who contends that the Bible supports racial segregation and discrimination. Wilful and uninformed people have sought to use the Bible as an aid in their mistaken support of segregation, but they have distorted the true meaning of the Scriptures. The Old Testament states over and over again in unmistakable language that there is "a fundamental unity of mankind in origin, nature and experience, in sinfulness and mortality and in the moral and spiritual laws to which men are subject. . . . In the New Testament the revelation in Christ abolishes the distinction and unites Jew and Gentile in one religious community. . . . The universalism of Christianity is based on the unique relation in which each individual stands to God. . . . No nation or race is answerable to itself but must discharge its duties with a sense of responsibility toward other nations and races."[3]

We have tried to cite here some of the obstacles to racial harmony that loom large in the thinking of people in this country. Despite the findings of psychologists, economists, and other social scientists engaged in exposing the unreality of our fears, it is not with these aspects that we as Christians are finally concerned. We rejoice in all the help coming from the social scientists. They supply resources we necessarily use. But there is a more fundamental problem, and to that we now turn.

CHRISTIANITY AND RACE

Racial prejudice in any and all forms is contrary to the will and design of God. Racial prejudice with the long series of unhappy incidents that flow from it is not merely bad, unfortunate, unrighteous—it is sin. Let this teaching be proclaimed. He who wrongs his brother sins against God.[4]

Every major church conference of recent years has dealt with the problem of race. These sentences do not summarize the entire Christian attitude toward race, but they point to the heart of the problem: racial prejudice is sin.

Possibly one of the reasons American church people have been reluctant to recognize the larger meaning of the term "sin" is that it includes whatever alienates us from God. This places a much greater demand upon our intelligence and conscience than the identification of sin with card-playing, dancing, or smoking.

Or, again, perhaps because sin implies a judgment upon us and takes away from us the prerogative of determining what is right and wrong, we have preferred to overlook it. Through choosing to "accentuate the positive" and emphasize our love toward God, we may have chosen to select the ways in which we exhibit our love toward God.

Whatever may have been our reasons for avoiding the reality of what is sinful, the fact remains that in our religious life conformity to the practices of our community and society have often taken precedence over any fear of sinfulness.

But love toward God and one's fellow men can never be something negative, something done unwillingly and under compulsion. Our Lord's summarizing of the Great Commandment involved a positive and voluntary response. Christ created a community among men, a fellowship of those who love him and are bound together by him in faith, hope, and love. In his fellowship human divisions that separate man from man have no place.[5] Some have attempted to show that this fellowship was never meant to be taken literally, that it is of a spiritual nature and does not involve actual social contact with those unlike ourselves. Such perversion of the Gospel's meaning has wrought world-wide havoc. God is the Father of all mankind and in Christ he redeemed not merely a single section of humanity. Acceptance of this redeeming act of God carries with it the willingness to disavow any exclusiveness.

The meaning for mankind of Christ's death upon the Cross is lost upon those of us who do not realize that God's act cannot be conveniently fractured to meet the whims of individuals.

John Knox suggests, in a similar vein though perhaps on a more personal level, "Nothing is clearer than that he [Christ] refused to interpret in racial terms the Kingdom of God in which he believed history would be shortly ended and fulfilled. God for him was the Father of all men."[6] No theme recurs more constantly in the Gospels than that of Christ's compassion for the underprivileged, the poor, the outcast, and the leper and his disregard of, indeed his anger at, the conventions that would separate him from those who most needed his help.

If the whole record in the Old and New Testaments of God's relationship to his people is analyzed, there is no alternative to the fact that God is the Father of all mankind, without discrimination.

But the churches established to serve one common Lord have frequently chosen to disavow the purposes and intention of the Lord they would serve. It is in the church, the fellowship within which Christ's spirit seeks to live and find expression, that a tragic blind spot exists. Belatedly, however, we are coming to recognize our wilfulness and failure. From innumerable sources, both Protestant and Catholic, come acknowledgments of penitence. One sentence from the latter is illustrative: "The church is not racist—indeed she is the antithesis of racism; she stands for the unity of the human family, yet for a unity which does not exclude diversities but rather comprehends them because it is 'Catholic.' "[7]

Some of the things the church has actually done about this problem will be considered later. Here we are trying to suggest briefly the inescapable demands upon any persons or institutions that would seek to be Christian.

It is through the Christian church that men come to know their ultimate hope and their common destiny. For this reason the church itself can know no bounds. True, there must be units of the church in varying geographical areas where different languages are spoken. But this is not the same as a divided church. Actually such area and national churches are but instruments to make known more widely this common hope. And one of the final tests of a church's authenticity is its capacity to open men's eyes to their oneness in Christ.

THE SCORE: LOSSES

Before listing some of the gratifying gains in fellowship we must mention places where losses are still to be registered.

Montgomery, Alabama, has received world-wide attention and has acquired a significance for our era which may convey prophecy and hope. It is included here on the "loss" side of the ledger because gain, though substantial, only points to a deficit. In a presumably religious nation, a law and custom exists that compels a woman to give her seat in a bus to a man just because of a color difference. It approximates barbarism if not inhumanity. In Montgomery the barbaric custom was challenged not by rioting but by the peaceful means of "boycott." This will bring a wholly unexpected renown to the city that is for many a symbol of a culture.

As these words are being written three hundred policemen are standing guard over a few square blocks containing a public housing project in the city of Chicago. For two years this number of policemen and sometimes many more have been guarding and attemping to maintain order in the same area. Violent hostility broke out when a Negro family moved into this housing project built with public funds. The forces fostering the violence were motivated by the same hate, distrust, and resentment held by other persons in many parts of the United States and other lands as well.

In the summer of 1955 a group of colored and white church leaders met on the campus of a college in Wadley, Alabama, to discuss the role of the church in world affairs. They had just discussed "United States Foreign Policy since 1945" and were about to unite in a closing worship service when they were ordered out of the community by a gang. A member of the group wrote, "We thought our major job was to combat undemocratic forces in Europe, Asia and the Near East. We discovered, however, that terrorism can be used right here in Wadley, U.S.A."[8] The editors of *Pravda* will probably smile when they read the story; and they will, no doubt, pass it along to the people we hope to win over to democracy.

One Sunday in December, 1952, a man named Nelson Cornelius went into an Indianapolis restaurant near the YMCA where he was a guest and sat down at a table. At first he was completely ignored, and later the manager told him he could not be served. As he rose to go, he said, "I am sorry—I have come a long way—10,000 miles." On further inquiry the manager learned he was from India and was not an American of African descent. He was then urged to stay and be served.[9]

Many readers will remember vividly the refusal of the Daughters of the American Revolution to allow one of America's greatest singers permission to share her talents with a mixed audience in their auditorium. Fortunately, a Secretary of the Interior who understood the meaning of Americanism made it possible for Marian Anderson to sing outdoors in front of the Lincoln Memorial. Miss Anderson's graciousness in the face of an insult and a denial of Americanism was an inspiration to all. True Americans rejoiced when Miss Anderson was invited to become a member of the Metropolitan Opera Company.

Frank Loescher has described in detail the kinds of segregation prevailing in Protestant churches. These range from mild suggestion to official restriction.[10] One of the most offensive church situations was eliminated when, in 1956, the Methodist General Conference voted to abolish its all-Negro "Central Jurisdiction" so that negroes might choose the local church of their preference.

Best known, perhaps, of all the troublesome situations involving race in the United States is the response of certain southern states to the desegregation decision of the Supreme Court. The bitter hostility to an enforcement of the American creed reveals such a weakness in the armor of both democracy and the cause of freedom that further comment is unnecessary.

These examples of faulty race relations are included lest we as Christians become anesthetized to actual conditions in the United States.

THE SCORE: GAINS

Benjamin Mays, president of Morehouse College, Atlanta, Georgia, sums up the gains made in American race relations in a comparison of the difference in conditions between 1936 and 1953. Between those two dates it became possible for Negroes to vote in all states of the South, even in rural areas and small towns. It became possible for them to ride in unsegregated coaches; to eat without the despicable green curtain which had come to symbolize segregation in the dining cars; to hold positions as clerks, buyers, and managers of department stores; and to study in many southern universities from which they had been excluded. In addition, as every American boy knows, the Big League baseball teams began to sign up Negro ball players, a move that began with Jackie Robinson. Both the teams and the gate receipts have improved as a result.[11]

It would be difficult to appraise the far-reaching implica-

97

tions of desegregation in the armed forces. Lee Nichols reports that by 1953 "the racial barrier had been virtually wiped out in the Air Force and in the Navy outside the almost entirely Negro stewards branch. The Army was far along the road to elimination of its all-Negro units."[12]

Alan Paton, author of Cry, the Beloved Country, was commissioned by Collier's magazine to look at race relations, its gains and losses, and to make a report. Lucidly and informally, he describes the integration in the armed forces and in many other phases of American society.

At one time a Negro soldier was first a Negro and only after that a soldier. But there were tales of his death and heroism; some enjoyed the experiences of his companionship and his unselfishness. The fact of his willingness to die for America so wounded the conscience of his country that his inferiority became unendurable. It was a thing no longer to be borne when an inferior man died a superior death.[13]

The statistics for Negro labor union membership would be out of date so quickly that there would be no point in recording them even if they could be accurately secured. Nevertheless, one of the brighter aspects of the American racial picture is the increasing number of unions willing to include Negroes in their membership. Unions are composed of the same people who make up our schools, churches, and other community organizations, and it is not surprising that the Negro has not been welcomed any more eagerly into the union brotherhoods. But labor unions have helped create an effective bulwark against discrimination. Before the merger of the AFL and the CIO, Willard Townsend, a highly respected labor leader, said that the CIO had helped to make Negro labor the most articulate section of the Negro population. As a group, they were better able to meet the problems of their race.[14]

Economically, the American Negroes have certainly gained. In 1951 they spent $15 billion, which was more than the national income of Canada. The average income of Negroes tripled from 1940 to 1950, while that of white citizens increased only one and one-half times in the same period.[15]

And so the record accumulates. The greatest and most far-reaching action of all, however, is the Supreme Court's decision on May 17, 1954, that racial segregation in the public schools of the nation is not constitutional. To that decision was added on June 30 the implementing opinion requiring that "the defendants make a prompt and reasonable start toward full compliance" with the ruling.

In the words of Alan Paton, "The remnants of segregation are doomed. . . . Just as America has accepted and made part of herself all the peoples of Europe and has resolved within herself those tensions which twice have torn the world apart, she now accepts or is on the threshold of accepting all those other races which live upon her soil. If she can now resolve within herself those tensions which could tear the world apart again how much greater her contribution to the world."[16]

It is into this situation that the full weight of the church's influence may be brought in the interest of the well-being of all God's children.

WHAT THE CHURCH HAS DONE

The role of the church in eliminating slavery constitutes one of the most thrilling chapters in church history. On American soil this battle was not waged without tragic loss in brotherhood. Some of the wounds are not yet healed. The story of the church's work deserves much space and attention. We will, therefore, have to confine our treatment of this theme to recent times.

Pronouncements by individual churches and denominations and by co-operating denominations may not be a true index of the extent of conviction among the members.

99

THE RESPONSIBLE CHRISTIAN

Nevertheless, they constitute a clue to the trends of thinking. Many of the ecumenical conferences held prior to the
Oxford conference on life and work in 1937 expressed a
Christian concern for and judgment upon practices injurious to people in all lands. The report of the Oxford
conference of 1937 said that the existence of various races,
black, white, and yellow, "is to be accepted gladly and
reverently." Trying to differentiate the races according to
their intrinsic value is completely inappropriate. All were
created by God "to bring their unique and distinctive contribution to His service in the world." The church is responsible for demonstrating the reality of God's community. It is "commissioned to call all men . . . into a divine society that transcends all national and racial limitations and divisions."[17] The fact that this conference was held
just before the guns began to fire in World War II and
coincided with the rise of Hitler and his attack upon certain racial groups gave added point to its utterances.

Immediately upon the close of World War II the Federal Council of Churches of Christ in America issued a
statement that has been quoted widely and incorporated in
subsequent statements including that of 1952 (when the
organization, had become the National Council of
Churches of Christ in the U.S.A.). It recommended that
member churches renounce segregation based on race,
color, or national origin as "a violation of the gospel of
love and human brotherhood. While recognizing that historical and social factors make it more difficult for some
churches than for others to realize the Christian ideal of
non-segregation the Council urges all of its constituent
members to work steadily and progressively toward a non-
segregated church."[18]

Almost all major denominations have their own statements about the theological basis for race relations and for
the conduct of the life of the church. Some denominations

have been more aggressive in their attempt to resolve this issue than others. Reasons for this difference may lie in the historic backgrounds of the various denominations.

Increasingly, both Catholic and Protestant churches are encouraging participation by all racial groups. This did not come about until a great many churches, formerly all-white, had sold their buildings after their congregations had moved to other areas. It became apparent that flight was no answer to the fundamental problem. More important was the development of a strategy for integrating all groups. Integration is by no means universal, but it has become so common that it would be unfair to single out individual congregations that have pioneered in this delicate but important new venture.

S. Garry Oniki in 1950 described a number of types of interracial churches. He quoted, for example, a description of an East Harlem parish that found a means of demonstrating the church's inclusiveness.[19] Since the writing of his account, however, at least three other such experiments have developed in major metropolitan centers, and the number of interracial churches has increased so greatly that there is no accurate record of the total. The Department of Racial and Cultural Relations of the National Council of Churches of Christ reported in 1951 a sampling of three Protestant denominations totaling 13,597 churches. Of these there were 1,331 predominantly white churches reporting non-white persons in their Christian fellowship as members or attendants. An infinitesimally small number of persons was reported to have left the churches because of the expansion of the circle of Christian fellowship. Among the many who remained, the ministers reported, there was greater fellowship and increased spiritual insight.[20]

It must not be presumed, however, that merely opening the membership of the churches to all races will bring about a more even division of races in the constituency of each church. In the Protestant conception of a local church individuals select the fellowship with which they would like to affiliate. The removal of the barrier to membership because of racial background, however, destroys another of the cancerous and strangling forces that injure the souls of those restricted. This is one of the revealing discoveries made in a study of both segregated and inclusive churches in Chicago.[21]

Many states have sought legal devices for circumventing the Supreme Court's decision on segregation. Some have declared the schools to be private and others have aided families that wished to send their children to other than an integrated school. The state of Virginia chose the latter device in a vote on the Gray Amendment, but there were many church people who went on record, through speeches and writings, against it "in a quietly bold defense of human dignity and Christian principle."[22]

There is desired and there must be the same opportunities and absence of restrictions in the church as are sought elsewhere. Negroes naturally want the same opportunities to work and get ahead as white people have. But they also want the little restrictions removed, too: "colored" signs on waiting rooms and drinking fountains and rules in buses, trains, and hotels. Bill Gordon, managing editor of the *Atlanta Daily World*, has said, "No, I don't want my son to marry a white girl. But I also don't like having to explain to him, when he's six or seven, why he's got to move to the back of the bus. These are the things that wear down your nerves."[23] Religious people should possibly be the first to understand what this means and to give it full opportunity for expression.

NOW, WHAT DO CHRISTIANS DO?

The Mohammedan religion accepted all colors and racial groups with little discrimination. Perhaps this was partly because it considered the non-Moslem to be outside the brotherhood of man. With conspicuous exceptions, Christianity has not been so hard on the non-Christian, but it has allowed racial discrimination to flourish. Even churchmen who lead movements for racial equalitarianism have congregations that are not practicing brotherhood. In 1943 Robert Redfield said that the revolution in Russia reduced racial discrimination there. "Where social categories are broken down by revolution or overwhelmed by some more important category, *as a religion of brotherhood*, race may lose its social importance in whole or in part."[24] If Redfield is correct, only a revolution or "a religion of brotherhood" may diminish the tragedy of racial hostility.

One cannot but ask the disturbing question: Is it because Christianity has lost its revolutionary quality that the notion of brotherhood has likewise disappeared? The facts would seem to support this conclusion.

Obviously, a mere knowledge of the facts is insufficient to change the fundamental conditions. Knowledge in itself rarely accomplishes anything. Racial attitudes—good or bad—are the product of emotional experiences. A wrong attitude, therefore, has the chance of being changed only if a satisfactory experience in another direction is made possible. This the church can help provide. Surely no institution should be better equipped for it, since the changing of attitudes is one of the church's chief purposes. Acquaintance is an indispensable requirement of harmonious relations, and the church by its very nature should excel in accomplishing this.

True, we must *know* first, but then there follows action. We are familiar with some of the reasons the church has been quiescent in the matter of race and prejudice. We know that we have not been sufficiently realistic about its sinfulness. But undercutting the cause of such prejudice involves us in vigorous activity.

103

Circumstances are forcing all respecters of human rights to participate in such activity. Just as the encroachment of juvenile delinquency on areas where people had thought themselves quite protected has made many people much more intelligent about the issue of juvenile delinquency, or as the impairment of our national strength by segregation in the armed forces necessitated our doing away with what contributed to weakness, so have we discovered, to our sorrow, that where the rights of any are threatened the rights of all are insecure. These facts we wish all people would know. But when religious individuals, and Christians in particular, give evidence of knowing such facts the eyes and ears of others may be opened likewise.

There are some hopeful signs on the horizon. Reference was made earlier to the statements from national and international religious organizations. It has become apparent that these are problems for the church. When a large company of ministers went into the office of the mayor of America's second largest city to protest housing discrimination, the mayor turned quietly to them and said, "How many of your churches are unsegregated?"

In this immediate period it is, of course, the issue of segregation which is making the headlines. Decisions of the Supreme Court and of many lesser courts are bolstering the efforts of those desiring justice and decency in human relations. The basic decision is not fundamentally a legal one; nevertheless, we can rejoice that the law of the land is undergirding what is right. But, as in the elimination of slavery, the work of the church must continue in the eradication of segregation. This is bluntly reiterated in Race Relations Sunday message of the National Council of Churches: "The churches are called upon to recognize the urgent necessity of taking a forthright stand on this crucial issue. If we are to remain true to the Gospel of Jesus Christ we must not rest until segregation is banished from every area of American life."[25]

Today the church is not the only organization that is helping to eliminate this festering sore in society. Education, the press, sports, labor, and some of the professions have also assisted. Some of this work is the outgrowth of economic pressure. Some of it results from the earnest convictions of religious laymen. But the struggle is only fairly begun. The outcome will determine whether the revolutionary understanding and action of the Christian faith will prove more effective in the hands of Christ's followers than the appeal of Mohammedism or the revolution of communism.

The problems of race, difficult as they are and insoluble as they sometimes appear, provide Christians with an opportunity for obedience and for a deeper understanding of the fact that slaves and freemen, Jews and Gentiles, and men of every land and continent are one in Christ.[26]

CHAPTER VI

COMMUNISM

American Christians and non-Christians wish that the spec-
ter of communism would wither away. Obviously this is
not happening and in all probability will not happen. To
halt the advance of this political system, which at the same
time has marked religious aspects, the United States has engaged in a program unprecedented in scope and cost. In so
doing we have frequently resorted to the very devices of
communism itself. Our misunderstanding of communism
has led us to use tactics that play into the opponent's
hands. Even more serious perhaps is the lack of confidence
in the resources of our national heritage. And for those of
the Judeo-Christian tradition it should be apparent that the
religious ideology of communism represents a distortion of
their understanding of man, a distortion not to be defeated
by still other distortions. It was not until many freedoms
had already been impaired and some of our priceless heritage corrupted that saner minds and wills began to prevail.
The temptation to oversimplify and to find easy scape-
goats when the more profound meanings and depths of
the evils we deplore cannot be identified is, of course, a
universal tendency. Naïvely, perhaps, it was thought by
some that legislation and force could remove communism.
Try as hard as we could with military might some eight
hundred million people in the Far East have come under
the aegis of this virile movement. In our own land freedom
of information, federal laws, a dynamic, free labor movement, and other forces have helped hold in check and reduce the influence of communism. Likewise, the extent to
which a vigorous economy is responsible cannot be over-
estimated. Presumably, there is a connection among all
these facts. Their implications for the rest of the world we
shall consider shortly.

It is because communism is a religion inseparably involved in and supporting an economic system that we are compelled to compare it with Christianity. The latter is not identified with any one economic system but has, nevertheless, exercised profound influence upon practices that are a part of the system designated as "capitalism." Among the individuals and nations opposed to and perhaps defeated by communism there has been an inclination to insist that the two religions stand in competition with each other as rsepective sustainers of economic orders.

But no devoted Communist would acknowledge that his faith was a religion. This is partly because communism's chief prophet, Karl Marx, denounced religion (with a phrase coined by a Christian minister, Charles Kingsley: "Religion is the opium of the people"). Despite demurrings from the disciples of Marx, however, the Communist's faith, by any criterion one could reasonably apply, is a religion. It offers a means of salvation, a world view, a total philosophy of life; writings of its chief prophet, Marx, are accorded ultimate authority; principal interpreters are held in utmost veneration—Lenin, and until recently, Stalin; a devil exists in the form of those who subscribe to the theory of private property—the bourgeoisie. And, finally, the Communist believes that the forces of righteousness are on his side and that he will ultimately be victorious.

But it is precisely because the Christian faith is not identified with an economic system that much of the confusion and misunderstanding his arisen regarding the way in which these two religious faiths relate themselves to the world scene.

In chapter i we referred briefly to the influence of the Judeo-Christian faith upon political systems emerging in the Western world. Those systems were given an indelible imprint from beliefs about the nature of man as found in that faith. Out of the understanding of man's destiny and meaning political revolutions took place. They caused these convictions about man and his worth to be written into constitutions and laws. It is significant, therefore, that in the land out of which communism comes and in which the doctrines of Karl Marx have been tried, no such revolution has ever occurred. The voices of Hebrew and Christian prophets have either been unheard or unheeded. This is not to say, of course, that there was no church. The term "Holy Russia" was current a century before the arrival of Lenin. It is a common observation that the violence of the Russian Revolution and its aftermath was the greater because the priesthood of this land had never fostered the "liberal" understanding of man such as saturated the intellectual revolutions in Europe and America.

Communism arose, thus, in the vacuum created by the absence from the church of a full expression of the Christian faith. It is no wonder, then, that the Communist leaders refuse to allow their people to know that there is such a breadth and depth to the Christian faith.

WHAT IS COMMUNISM?

Much of the hysteria over communism is fostered by a lack of understanding of what communism is. The charge that it is atheistic cannot always be said to stem from a genuine devotion to theism, certainly not to the God who is the Father of our Lord Jesus Christ. Nor is the designation of communism as the destroyer of democracy founded, always, on a devotion to democratic principles. Many opponents of communism have been quite willing to sabotage democracy in the process of their attack of communism.

What, then, really is this ideology and faith called communism? There is no simple, single, brief definition that can do justice to the vastness of the communist position. One analyst of this political-religious faith says: "Communism, at least according to classical theory, aims at creating a classless society in which all the means of production, distribution and exchange will be owned by the community and from which the state—conceived as an instrument of coercion and oppression—will have disappeared."[1] At least this is the way the intellectual formulator of communism, Karl Marx, intended it should be. But, obviously, Soviet communism has deviated from this prescription. Though it may be expected that the state will wither away, it is quite apparent that the present determiners of communist policy have moved in exactly the opposite direction. The communist state has actually increased its structure and power.

Another phase of Marx's thesis is that all history is the history of the struggle between the class owning nothing—the proletariat—and the class owning something—the bourgeoisie, including small and great businessmen and independent farmers. "The class which owns nothing, the proletariat, is engaged in a death struggle with the class which owns something, the bourgeoisie; and Marx holds that the bourgeoisie must inevitably lose the struggle."[2]

True, Marxism is not the sum total of Soviet communism. Lenin, the great effecter and strategist of the Marxist communist state, modified the Marxism of 1848 to make it applicable to the twentieth century. Subsequently, Stalin and those who with him directed the destinies of Soviet Russia also made modificaions. Nevertheless, the fundamental pattern still prevails.

Communism claims to provide the only order built around the scientific analysis of society. Religions are outmoded in the communist point of view because they are prescientific. Obviously, in an era when science determines so large a part of man's life, an assumption that a political order is based on scientific "truth" carries weight.

Communism offers release from the shackles of economic control by those who, according to their theory, are responsible for keeping men in subjection and poverty. The new and perfect order of human society will be created here and now and need not await some far-off intervention by an unknown deity. The new order is the classless and propertyless society where the human tragedies caused by disparity in wealth and possessions are eliminated.

The devil in the present world situation is the institution of capitalism and the economic order created around it. Presumably, if this demon could be exorcised, the good in men would have opportunity to come out and the perfect order of mankind would be achieved.

To a degree unattained by any other nation in the history of the world, a backward, second-class nation with a predominantly peasant population has come to the fore and in twenty years attained the position of one of the two most powerful nations in existence. Such a demonstration is very convincing to other peoples of the world who have also lagged behind the procession in the use of scientific methods in their industrial and economic life. It is not difficult to understand why the people of underdeveloped areas are responsive to leaders who point to the extraordinary achievement of another nation that not long ago was only slightly better off.

Quite rightly people say that what communism was, either in its original formulation by Marx and his colleague, Engels, or through the additions made by Lenin, does not adequately represent what communism has become. The capitulation of China to communism, the attempted conquest of South Korea, and the gains made elsewhere in Southeast Asia announce that the militant aggressiveness of communism is more than merely a set of ideas held by a few strategists. Such a driving conviction as dominates the life and thought of communist leaders—and followers—cannot be contained in a single area. It is the fact that communism must expand and include ever increasing populations, tying them economically and spiritually to the Soviet Union, that gives pause and anxiety to the West. The basis of its appeal lies in the promises of a great new future, a classless society, and a rejection of those who now possess power. Emancipation from economic slavery and degradation is universally appealing.

The eager portrayal of every instance of discrimination in America attests to another powerful appeal of communism among dark-skinned peoples. Whereas capitalism and Christianity are assumed to be closely identified with the white populations, communism makes no distinction, theoretically. This fact provides leverage and a basis of appeal in that portion of the globe which is almost entirely composed of non-white peoples.

Communism is thus a total theory of life, built upon the age-old expectation of a new and perfect order, utilizing the skills and technical advancements of the modern era, promising a release from suffering caused by the domination of others, and guaranteeing a new brotherhood unhindered by race or property.

Obviously, military and economic warfare is no more likely to defeat such a powerful religio-economic movement than was Constantine in the fourth century able to suppress the rising tide of Christian conviction. Before turning, however, to the specifically Christian analysis and counterproposal, we must see what the West has offered as a counterbalance to the economic salvation in the communist proposals.

COMPETITION BETWEEN COM-
MUNISM AND THE WEST

Economic conditions are a primary condition in the spread of communism. "Babies are the most prolific crop in most Asiatic and African countries today. Population is increasing by millions every year—far more rapidly than the supply of wheat or rice; and communism thrives on an empty stomach." In such countries, interest in communism "is more a protest against harsh living conditions than positive enthusiasm for communistic ideas."[3] So observes one of the advisers with our occupation forces in Japan. Statements like his are repeated on all sides. A catalogue of the inroads made by communist propagandists and political agents all through Southeast Asia bears an almost monotonous repetition. It is the same story from nation to nation.

Few persons have had a better opportunity to observe the communist advances and the reasons for them than Chester Bowles, our former ambassador to India. He has described the way in which Soviet power has penetrated Egypt and become a major political factor in the Middle East. Likewise, in India shrewd effort is being made to develop closer relationships. In Burma and in the crown colony of Singapore the situation grows steadily more inflammable.

In Japan a large-scale movement has come into being; the continent of Africa in all parts is alive with communist activity. At this writing communist infiltration of Egypt and other Arab countries has already resulted in bloodshed, sorely damaged the economic and political life of England and France, and brought many other nations to the "brink of war."

It is not only in the underdeveloped portions of the world that communism possesses power. It has been strong enough in France to impede the achievement of a stable government there. Even in solidly Roman Catholic Italy, Soviet-affiliated agents have been capable of checking the plans of major parties. But, significantly, in the lands where the Christian understanding of the nature of man and of society has found expression in and has been implemented by the political systems, communism has made no extensive headway. This does not mean that it will not be able to make such headway in the future. It simply implies that a combination of factors, among them the impact of the Christian faith upon political life, has provided an effective barrier to communism's spread.

Bowles sums up his plea for a more realistic appraisal of the worldwide communist situation with a reminder that "it cost America and her allies tens of thousands of lives and more than fifty billion dollars in equipment to keep the communists out of South Korea. If we stumble now we may be forced to pay a vastly higher price to keep them out of Europe, the Middle East, South Asia and Africa. The measure of our response should be its adequacy to the new Soviet challenge. Let it not be said by future historians that in the second decade after World War II freedom throughout the world died of a balanced budget."[4]

The Bowles appeal is not limited to financial assistance or economic measures, as all know who were aware of his extraordinary influence while serving as ambassador. We are aware that economic and military aid is indispensable. But they are the tools of something else—they cannot be ends or purposes in and of themselves.

The critique of communism and the alternatives to it, if they are to be effective, must be contained in an ideology and a faith that is more real and more persuasive than what communism offers. British economist Barbara Ward is one of those who has been reminding the West of its more powerful instruments of persuasion. The Russian appeal is not economic so much as it is poetic. "To devote oneself to ridiculing their economic view of history is a waste of time. They have no such thing." For underdeveloped areas, it is we who are the economic men, and it is up to us to prove that we are something more than profit-and-loss

113

experts; we must prove we have "some spark in our soul of the infinite spirit of man."[5]

Two years later, after a trip around the world, Miss Ward wrote of the paradox of communism itself. The "poets" who had talked of brotherhood, love, and the creation of a new world reproduced "an Asiatic despotism of the most alarming power and brutality."[6] Thus an economic movement clothed in religious phraseology with its hope for a messianic era ends with the enslavement and degradation of countless numbers of persons who, either out of falsely inspired hope or from fear of being swept up in a tide of revolution, were brought to disillusion and despair.

It would be naïve to assume that the contest between the two great powers, Russia and the United States, would be resolved and that harmony would be restored if the issue could be spelled out in its most fundamental form with a realistic religious analysis. Politics does not yield to anything so simple. Nevertheless, even though the issues have been long in formulating and are unspeakably complicated, the fact remains that basically they are spiritual in nature—that is, they are determined by man's understanding of himself, his role in life, and his own ultimate destiny. Because the Christian faith speaks primarily to such a condition and is involved with the kinds of economic orders men create for themselves, we turn to the Christian faith for its contribution to this world dilemma.

THE CHRISTIAN ANALYSIS
AND ALTERNATIVE

Far too much energy has been expended by Christians on a defense of Christianity in the face of the extensive gains of communism. The reason for this primary concern with defense instead of with a powerful expression of the Christian faith itself would make an interesting analysis.

It is surely not wholly wide of the mark to suggest that because Christians have themselves been so unfamiliar with the deeper insights of their inherited faith they have not felt free to confront other men with it. Or, again, perhaps Christians have been so content to rely upon the security of the Western economic system that they have not felt it necessary to examine the presuppositions about the nature of man underlying Western political structures. Another reason for this reluctance to express the Christian faith is, presumably, the many diverse interpretations of faith in Christendom. The combination of these and other factors have, no doubt, contributed to Christians' confusion about their relationship to communism. Thus they have been tempted to strike out with more heat than light and have given unwitting aid to the secular emotionalists who have nothing better to offer than to "stop communism."

The way in which China was quickly overrun by communist forces provides a good illustration of the ineffectiveness of a narrow Christian faith against communist propaganda. There, earnest Christian students were forced "to defend their faith in terms of Genesis versus the origin of species, instead of at some higher more worthy level." In the midst of a scientific and technological revolution "the church cannot refute scientism by an ostrich pose. Those who . . . deny all advance in modern thought might just as well try to solve the problem of thermo-nuclear power by denying its existence. They are fit topics for Soviet caricature."[7]

There is a pseudoreligious appeal often made to Christians and likewise used as a Christian argument for stopping communism. It is the assumption that the Christian faith values the individual and respects his dignity, while communism values the state and subordinates the individual to the collective. Reinhold Niebuhr considers this a "pathetic perversion" of Christianity and a serious misinterpretation of communism. "It is, however, so prevalent that thousands of sermons are preached on this particular theme. . . . It is significant that the same culture which prated so monotonously about the 'dignity of man' frequently comes up with a picture of man in which he is the mere creature of a natural or historical process and has lost all responsibility for his action."[8]

Churches and Christianity, in the minds of some people, are to be used as tools to oppose communism. When religious leaders have protested this misuse of the church and the Christian faith, they have been accused of disloyalty or of a lack of genuine devotion to Christianity. Such suspicion could arise only out of a misunderstanding of the nature of the faith which forms the church. The Christian faith is not a device to be used in the service of any system of ideas or any particular social order.

What, then, is the fundamental distinction between these two rival faiths? The Amsterdam Conference of the World Council of Churches summarized the points of conflict between Christianity and communism as follows: (1) Communists promise what amounts to a complete redemption of man in history. (2) Communists believe that a particular class, by virtue of its role as the bearer of a new order, is free from the sins and ambiguities that Christians believe to be characteristic of all human existence. (3) The materialistic and deterministic teachings of communism, however they may be qualified, are incompatible with belief in God and with the Christian view of man as a person made in God's image and responsible to him. (4) The ruthless methods of Communists in dealing with their opponents are incompatible with Christianity. (5) Finally, the Communist party demands of its members an exclusive and unqualified loyalty which, in the Christian view, belongs only to God. The communist dictatorship attempts to control every aspect of life.[9]

To the Christian, man does not determine the ends of history. He is not the final judge of what takes place in his life. All life belongs to God. It is his order and man constantly stands under God's judgment for what he does with the life intrusted to him.

No one class of people can be held responsible for the ills of the world. Neither can capitalism or any other institution be charged with all the harm that has been done to mankind. The Kingdom of God, which has played so large a role in the history of Christian thought, cannot be thought of as merely a classless society. It is rather the era that prevails in man's heart when they accept the rule of God. As Alexander Miller has said: "There is a universe of difference between the testimony that history will have a verdict delivered on it . . . and the view which sets the end of history within itself."[10] No order is free from sinfulness.

Christianity is not an other-worldly religion in the sense that it is not concerned with the things of this world. It is very much concerned with things in this world. But this concern is markedly different from the materialism of Marxian communism. Christianity insists that all the material realm of life is held in trust under God and that men are but stewards of the life they live and of their possessions. Man who uses these possessions is thus not finally responsible only to himself. Made as he is in the image of God, he is responsible to Him. The way he relates himself to his fellow men in the use of material things, however, is the truest test of his acknowledgment of God's sovereignty.

Starting with the assumption that all men are children of God, the Christian is deeply concerned over the kind of treatment accorded God's children. That they have not always been so concerned is grist for the communist mill and a part of the great tragedy of human experience. The

117

tragedy is compounded in the fact that much of the ill-treatment of others of God's children has been done in the name of religion under the impetus of the church. The term "community," which shares its root with the word "communism," is a fundamental Christian concept implying a oneness of men bound together by a common fatherhood and origin. The abuse of this infinitely far-reaching idea has opened the door for communism and made it possible.

Ultimate loyalty for the Christian can be centered only in one place—God. Where men's loyalties are centered in God as the author and creator of life and in Jesus Christ, totalitarian systems have found their stumbling block. Men who give their ultimate loyalty to God cannot give it to the state. To communism and fascism it is essential that absolute devotion be accorded to the state. For this reason, both communism and fascism have made it mandatory that the church be subject to the state. Until defeated militarily, Hitler was able to enforce this situation and until now communism has also been able to maintain itself.

Obviously, the communist concept of community and the Christian understanding of it are far apart. To the Christian the community is not merely a collection of individuals. The power of love transcends the possible cleavage between the person and the collective, making the person a loving and loved person and the community a community of persons, not of atoms. The Christian community is a fellowship bound together by a quality of life which is of a piece with God's relationship to man. This is revolutionary doctrine. It is applicable to all systems, including capitalism and communism. Up to now, in modern life at least, society has been held together by a power of social cohesion created through the "unofficial inheritance of Christian morality."[11] Now, under the powerful demonstration of Soviet communism, it becomes apparent that we can no longer automatically count upon these moral reserves for any economic system. It is precisely at this point that Christianity directs moral judgment upon the two great economic systems—and all the lesser ones.

A review of the fundamental convictions of the Christian faith and its Jewish origins almost invariably gives rise to the query, "Isn't there much in the communist faith which resembles the Christian faith and the order it would seem to inspire?" Many sage observers have been impressed with this fact. Oswald Spengler is author of the observation: "Christian theology is the grandmother of Bolshevism." A. William Loos contends that Spengler was referring to "the efforts of communism to minister to human welfare. Such efforts to achieve social justice stand in direct line with the teachings of the prophets and Jesus."[12] Likewise have such contemporary prophetic spirits as Jacques Maritain and the late Archbishop William Temple referred to communism as a "Christian heresy." John Bennett distinguishes the Christian hope for the Kingdom of God and the communist hope for the new order that will be established after the final triumph of the revolution in this way: the communist goal is a new society that will be fully established in history, whereas the Kingdom of God is a "source of judgment upon every social order."[13]

These differences in the understanding of the nature of community and of the final order of life, whether on this earth or beyond, are important. Yet there is another which stands out pre-eminently. It is the fact of Jesus Christ himself. To Christians the coming of Christ into the human scene is known as the "kerygma." It is by this fact and what it means to the Christian that all other events, systems, and loyalties are judged. The kerygma is the event of God's act in human history. The bringing of Jesus Christ to the life of man is the starting point and the final arbiter of all the Christian's acts. It is from this fact that man derives his understanding of God's relationship to other men and knows that ultimately all values lie within the nature and character of God. The kind of society toward which man is to work is a society reflecting such a quality and such a source.

This, finally, is the essence of the difference between communism and Christianity: the Christian's relationship to his Lord impels him to create a society where love and justice prevail, a society that stands in condemnation of any not thus founded.

It is possible that the indictment by Christians of the communist revolution and all it implies may be in part a device to ease their consciences for defaulting on the Christian revolution. For Christianity requires a continuous revolution. It is not so naïve as to assume that any political or economic system would fully embody what the Christian faith requires of men. The Christian revolution eternally reminds men of their tendency to rely on instruments and systems that will flatter them and dull their sensitivity to higher loyalties. It is this prior claim which communism, of course, rejects. But communism is not alone in its rejection. Communists know that Christians are vulnerable at this point, too. So the communist revolution has thrived on the Christians' failure to live their own revolution.

Thus for the Christian there are no built-in guaranties that the order of society he develops will supersede or win out over a society created by avowed antitheistic men. He has only the assurance that honest attempts to fulfil God's will, known or to be made known to him, will accord to his fellow men a fuller measure of what God intended for them. This is a far more profound and realistic revolution than one based on the class struggle or a so-called scientific view of man. For the Christian the lordship of Christ stands as a constant indictment of his pretensions and as the foundation of his hope.

120

CHAPTER VII

PUBLIC AND PRIVATE
WELFARE

A concern for human welfare growing out of our religious heritage is one of the things Americans take for granted. Meeting human need is a fundamental expression of religious heritage, and we assume that religious support underlies most welfare activity in this nation.

It is not easy for us to comprehend, therefore, the shift in emphasis that makes at least four-fifths of the welfare activity in the nation the responsibility of tax-supported, "secular" agencies. Perhaps one reason for this shift in philosophy regarding social welfare work is the assumption that the non-church welfare agencies are themselves deeply motivated by religion. The mode of transition is noteworthy.

F. Ernest Johnson has suggested: "Christianity may well be called the mother of social work in the western world. When Christianity became a dominant influence in western culture 'charity' in the original and noble sense of that word became a common ideal even where it fell short of being a common virtue. Thus it was possible for the church to inspire and guide philanthropic work under community as well as under parish auspices."[1]

The fact that the church and religious agencies could continue to "guide philanthropic work under community as well as under parish auspices" may help provide a key for the present state of the relationship between the church and public welfare in America today. In Colonial America church and community were in many areas synonymous. Then came the impact of industrialization and, with it, large-scale immigration, bringing to these shores people from other than Anglo-Saxon countries. Many different religious practices became established both in the settled portion of the country and on the frontier. But behind the movements of immigration was the industrial revolution itself, the real force and power making necessary a radically different concept of welfare.

Sensitive people, for the most part from religious backgrounds, undertook to alleviate some of the brutalities resulting from the type of economy that arrived with force in the nineteenth century. A partial catalogue of the ills that social work leaders sought to alleviate includes the mismanagement of prisons; the jailing of the insane and mentally defective; the abuse of convict labor; the inadequate care of children at home and in institutions; and child labor. In addition they fought against tuberculosis, alcoholism, industrial accidents, preventable infant mortality, illegitimacy, prostitution and the white slave trade, the practical bondage of victims of loan sharks, and slums and other overcrowded and disease-spreading housing.

But social workers, insofar as they knew how, also fought for something better than the alleviation of the worst social ills. They sought positive social good. First, they strove for better social casework, group work, and community organization, for better agency administration, and for social reform through enlightened public opinion and improved legislation. Then, they worked to orient and adjust immigrants, at the same time helping them to conserve their individual cultural gifts for the enrichment of American life. They organized new social settlements and placed children in adopting families or in foster homes. They helped obtain better legal protection against child labor, better sanitary and health safeguards through housing and building codes. They were an important force in the achievement of workmen's compensation programs, pensions for the needy aged, and unemployment insurance systems.[2]

This magnificent array of accomplishments cannot be

attributed wholly or even primarily to church activity. There were many individuals who, discouraged by the seeming sluggishness of the church's concern for human welfare, left the church and found their more satisfying relationships with other welfare workers. There are many who would now say that those pioneers in social welfare were closer to the real spirit of the church than were the institutions from which they felt it necessary to separate.

But, lest one judge the church too harshly, it must quickly be said that there were very few persons in or out of the church who comprehend the full scope of what was happening to American life and industrial life everywhere else in the world. Religion serves the function of helping to protect men against the vicissitudes of life, but it also helps them to understand and evaluate the changes correctly. These are known as the priestly and the prophetic function, respectively. Social work and pioneering on welfare fronts belong in the prophetic category.

No nation in history had ever gone down this path before. There were no guideposts to an industrial era. No nation in history had ever been confronted with the problem of assimilating thirty million immigrants. The ills that accompanied the industrialization of this nation could be met only by resources not yet devised. The church, ideally supposed to serve the total community, could not be adapted quickly enough to meet the avalanche of problems. No church had the resources to solve this kind of dilemma. All manner of panaceas were offered—some of them under religious auspices. Finally the great depression of the thirty's confronted us with the necessity of attempting to meet the problem all-inclusively rather than piecemeal.

The Social Security Act of 1935 was the largest and most inclusive attempt at meeting welfare needs yet undertaken by this nation. It is obviously useless to debate whether the humane aspects of that act were religiously motivated or were instituted to forestall revolution or to maintain a party in power. It may be significant that the two major nations that have maintained their stability in the modern world, England and the United States, are those whose political life is undergirded by a religious philosophy and whose religious life finds expression in democratic forms. In each case the well-being of the total community is justified and interpreted as a religious concern.

A brief résumé of the main provisions of the Social Security Act of 1935 reveals the extraordinary breadth of this single public welfare measure. It provides (1) a national system of Old Age and Survivors Insurance; (2) federal-state systems of unemployment compensation and of employment services; (3) federal grants to the states for public assistance; (4) federal grants to the states for maternal and child health services, to enable the states to extend and improve their programs, in rural areas especially; (5) federal grants to the states for services for crippled children, administered by the children's bureaus; and (6) federal grants to the states for child welfare services administered by the children's bureaus.

Before the Social Security Act, however, there had been in operation other federal activities such as (1) a system for payment of pensions and disability annuities to railroad employees, administered by the Railroad Retirement Board, established in 1935; (2) a school lunch program, consisting of grants to states for the benefit of pupils in both public and private schools; (3) the Office of Vocational Rehabilitation, which co-operates with the states in providing rehabilitation to persons in order to enable them to prepare for and to take their places in remunerative employment; and (4) the Veterans Administration, which extends major benefits to numerous war veterans.[3]

It would, obviously, be impossible in this brief space to list all the welfare services provided under public auspices.

Every state, county, and municipality operates extensive programs. In addition to federal and state benefits, many corporations have provided an increasing number of "fringe benefits," which include assistance during layoffs and following cessation of employment.

Private welfare agencies, often non-sectarian or unaffiliated with any one denomination, are partly financed by the Community Fund or Community Chest, the name of the organization depending on the kind of support rendered. These organizations are a means both of assuring efficiency and of reducing the frequency of campaigns by separate organizations. They provide assistance to welfare agencies of religious affiliation, also.

One outgrowth of this centralized financing of the welfare agencies, both secular and religious, has been the development of the welfare council, known by various names. Its purpose is to make certain that the welfare needs of a designated area are met, and with reasonable efficiency. To these councils can be credited no small measure of the raising of standards in religious agencies.

But this very condensed view of public welfare would be incomplete without reference to the development of the schools of social work. The administration of social welfare has become one of the indispensable professions in modern society. Its range is as broad as human need itself; it cares for the mentally disturbed child, the anxious aged, the sick, the hungry, the bereft, and those torn by imprisonment. It administers to the family and to all the other worthwhile institutions in society.

It is one of the interesting phenomena of American life that many of the persons trained in schools of social work are themselves children of the parsonage or have been deeply affected by their religion. Public welfare and its administration in America has been, thus far at least, markedly influenced by church and synagogue.

CHURCH WELFARE ACTIVITIES

As public welfare agencies increase in number and scope, an obvious question arises: What is the role of specifically religious social welfare activity? Are there aspects of social work that are now neglected or in need of special attention? During the period when the largest number of immigrants were being assimilated into American life, learning the language and customs and finding occupation, many church settlement houses provided untold services and benefits to these newcomers, regardless of their religious affiliation. The institutional church performed other services. It attempted to minister to people in congested areas, most of whom had no previous affiliation with the denomination supporting the institutional church. The church itself fulfilled many of the functions of a settlement house, attempting at the same time to make its religious influence felt. The intensity of its membership-recruiting program varied greatly even within a single denomination.

There is no complete census of Protestant social welfare agencies and institutions. Many welfare activities defy classification. Cayton and Nishi have attempted the most comprehensive census of such agencies and institutions thus far. They indicate that there are 2,783 health and welfare agencies and institutions related to 37 Protestant denominations that together account for over 70 per cent of the total Protestant church membership in the country.[4] The most important of these institutions are homes for the aged, hospitals, neighborhood houses, and institutions for the care of children. But there are church-related agencies in every field of welfare work. They constitute a large part of the churches' operations, but they do only a small proportion of all the social welfare work in the United States.[5]

Reference has been made to the development of the settlement house by Protestant denominations. The reason

126

for public awareness of this institution lies possibly in its dramatic appeal, dealing as it does with youth especially but providing opportunity for many age groups to develop their group life and individual skills. So many distinguished persons have come out of the settlement houses of America that it is unfair to single out any one person. City work departments of the various denominational and interdenominational religious organizations still find the settlement house and its modern adaptation an instrument of service to human need in the city.

But even more numerous than the settlement houses are the institutions that provide care to the aged. Spontaneously and simultaneously in different parts of the country there has emerged a wave of interest in the "senior citizens." Because so many people at this age are in churches and because of the increased longevity of Americans in general, the church has come to see that this group is one for which it can provide services in a very special way. The Social Security Act of 1935 has made possible an independence and a corresponding increase of self-respect for many of the older generation. It has become possible for them to reside in places of their own choosing, which can be a home set up by church agencies. Denominational funds have been made available to provide for their care. This has opened up a whole new vista of welfare possibilities in the life of the church.

At the other end of the age scale is the group for which the church has always had a special concern, namely, youth. The Protestant emphasis generally has not been upon an institutional program, and hence it has directly or indirectly given its support to the present-day trend of placing children in homes rather than in orphanages or other such institutions, whatever their name. There still remains a need for special institutions for children with particular ailments and others needing specialized care.

127

Deserving of highest praise—and of more space than these few pages allow—are, of course, the Young Men's and Young Women's Christian Associations. In a very real sense they perform religious social work with people of all ages, despite the word "young" in their titles. They are the product of the church's concern for a ministry to the whole person. Their leadership is church related and their purposes are akin to those of the major Protestant denominations. Because of their breadth of interest and scope of services they obviously cannot be affiliated with specific denominations. Nevertheless, there is no responsible YMCA or YWCA representative who would not identify these organizations with the church in its comprehensive purpose to serve human need.

Local councils of churches in communities large enough to support such councils have engaged in services designed to prevent delinquency or have ministered to those needing counseling and supervision. This type of pioneering service by Protestant agencies is in its infancy.

Even an abbreviated catalogue of social services rendered by the church would, of course, include the activities sponsored by Church World Service and the Christian Rural Overseas Program, the aid to refugees, and the activities originally carried on in co-operation with the Point Four program of the federal government. Such a catalogue would also include the work of the Institute of Pastoral Care and the Council for Clinical Training, Inc., which supply chaplains for institutions. It would also include the work done with migrants and American Indians in this country and the work with Puerto Ricans both in this country and in Puerto Rico.

In this book we can only suggest something of the range of work being done under church auspices. In each activity there is an element of pioneering, the church frequently undertaking work that public welfare may not yet be ready to do or perhaps should not do. In each church-sponsored agency, the personnel usually is of the caliber and has the training equal to that expected in the best professional circles of social work. Theological students interested in social work as a specific form of their ministry have often acquired social work training in one of the approved schools. In the present period there is a small but steady movement of theological students into schools of social work, and vice versa. The especially important aspect of all this, however, is the growing awareness on the part of those who desire to work specifically under church auspices of the necessity for superior training in social work. It has its counterpart in the growing interest on the part of social workers in the religious foundations of the work in which they are engaged, whether it be under public or private auspices.

MOTIVES FOR CHURCH PARTICIPATION

The preceding discussion indicates that many religiously motivated people are to be found in the ranks of so-called secular welfare workers. At the same time there are a great many fully trained and competent social workers employed by so-called religious agencies. These workers have been employed primarily because they possess the necessary training and skill to perform the tasks undertaken by their agencies. Many of these workers do not even belong to the denomination or acknowledge the particular faith sponsoring the agency. There are Protestant agencies which employ Catholic and Jewish social workers. For example, few social agencies enjoy a higher reputation for quality of work, efficiency, and understanding than does the Salvation Army. Yet the Salvation Army does not select its workers only from its own ranks. It demands capable and trained workers. This is not to imply that just any trained worker would be acceptable by those Protestant agencies; presumably he must also be a person of integrity. The point is

that religious agencies will not accept "dedicated ignorance" as a basis for social work leadership. Though this
policy may have cost various religious agencies some willing
and eager workers, it has improved the service rendered by
church-related institutions.

What, then, constitutes the basis for the churches' participation in social welfare activities? Some laymen have
not understood the insistence of the leaders of church
agencies on standards that seem higher than necessary.
Also, diligent church workers occasionally feel their agency
should be an instrument for the advancement of the
church's cause. Therefore, they have at times been reluctant to make full use of secular or non-religious agencies. A
zealousness for the church may create a situation in which
two separate values are involved—loyalty both to the ecclesiastical institution and to the social worker's ideal of efficiency.

At the very time that members of the social work profession have come to recognize the need for understanding
the deeper meaning of the work in which they are engaged,
church leaders have become aware of the fact that the
church has failed to confront society in general and its con-
stituents in particular with the profounder religious meaning of society itself. Symptomatic of this fact is the increasing tide of social work literature dealing with philosophical
issues and values. This awareness gave rise to the great conference on "The Church and Social Work" held in 1955 in
Cleveland, Ohio, and subsequently to "The National Conference on Policy and Strategy in Social Welfare" held in
1957 in Atlantic City, N.J.

In this chapter we have borrowed heavily from the material of the 1955 conference. One of the volumes prepared
for it is composed of a review of the kinds of social service
activities rendered by each of the major denominations and
a discussion of the reasons for their engaging in such pro-

grams and activities. As the editor suggests, "The churches are more alike in their practices in social welfare than in their reasons for them and more alike in their reasons than in their explanations of them."[6]

No single explanation of the religious foundations of social work would suffice for all the denominational statements, but there is, nevertheless, a very great measure of uniformity. Most churches engage in welfare work to express their love of God and man, to achieve justice as a fulfilment of love, to indicate acceptance of the prophetic emphasis in both the Old and New Testaments, to fulfil our Lord's injunctions as suggested in the parable of the Good Samaritan, to lift the level of human life in order that souls may be saved, to show their acceptance of the lordship of Christ, of his Kingdom, and of the primacy of biblical commands to serve one's neighbor, to express the love of God planted as a seed in each individual, to become a Christ to one's neighbor, and to recognize and acknowledge the sovereignty of God in all matters and to serve him in all things.

Additional reasons for the church to engage in social work were found by one group that specifically investigated the subject. First, there is the fellowship rooted in the Word of God, created in Holy Bapitsm, and sustained by Holy Communion. Then, there is the fact that social work provides for the church an organized medium for meeting human needs and for relating itself to the community, a means for relating the traditional spiritual therapy to the new therapies, and a source of information for a program of prevention and social action. Finally, it offers church members manifold channels for the expression of the Christian faith.[7]

Many are the ways in which these imperatives can be expressed and fulfilled. Fundamentally, they are all posited on the assumption of God's supremacy over all life and man's obligation to love and serve his fellow men as God has served him. Obviously, mingled with the purely "spiritual" purposes are motives for institutional advancement as well. Benefits accrue both to the doer and to the institution represented.

A census of the motives for church social work a century ago or perhaps even as recently as the beginning of the twentieth century would possibly reveal marked differences from today's motives. One reason for those differences is presumably the fact that injunctions derived from biblical sources have not always been sufficient to guarantee intelligent welfare service. A tendency to apply literally what in its origins apparently was never intended to be applied literally has made for confusion and often for sad consequences.

Coincident with the rise of the social welfare profession and the fuller awareness stemming from such disciplines as sociology and psychology there has been growing a much more comprehensive understanding of biblical theology. It has become apparent that the biblical insights regarding the nature of man and of society are of paramount value to anyone who would work with individuals and with the social order.

In one form or another the question has often been asked, "With all the knowledge we have of biblical content, why has there been so great a lag in applying the specific biblical injunctions to the society in which we live?" The Ten Commandments are explicit. In Deuteronomy, Psalms, and Proverbs men are enjoined to care for the needy. In the gospels men are instructed very plainly concerning their treatment of the injured, the imprisoned, the sick, and the defenseless.

The problem does not stem from unfamiliarity with the biblical commands and injunctions. Magnificent and far-reaching things have been done in response to these injunctions. They have lifted the level of humanity and brought healing and hope where there had been none. May

it be, though, that in the twentieth century the impetus to
genuine social welfare and reconstruction will have to depend upon motivation other than what was popularly assumed in another period to be found in the biblical injunctions? It is to this theme that we turn in the conclud-
ing paragraphs.

A PROTESTANT BASIS FOR SOCIAL WELFARE

Just as no one theological formulation would be acceptable to all religious groups engaging in welfare activities,
neither is there unanimity as to purpose and philosophy
among those directing public welfare. Nevertheless, there
is universal agreement that need must be met, that hunger
must be assuaged, that insecurity, insofar as it is humanly
caused, may be eliminated, that family disintegration
should be halted, that the injured of body and mind should
be healed.

The encouraging fact is that there are available in this
generation healing resources that have not been known or
as readily available hitherto. Deep in the American way of
life there is an assumption that all such beneficial resources
should be utilized rather than withheld. As Arnold Toynbee has observed, this conviction is rooted in American culture and thought; it grew out of a sudden acquisition of
immense new resources on the North American continent.
The spirit of the frontier engendered by this hitherto unex-
perienced situation disposed pioneers to develop customs
and practices of care for those in need. He thinks that "our
age will be remembered chiefly neither for its horrifying
crimes nor for its astonishing inventions, but for its having
been the first age since the dawn of civilization, some five
or six thousand years back, in which people dared to think
it practicable to make the benefits of civilization available
for the whole human race."[8] The question, therefore, is no

longer *whether* welfare resources shall be made available but *to what end.*

To no one institution or clique of secular or religious welfare leaders could the direction and planning of all welfare services be intrusted. It is the conviction of this writer, however, that all social work derives from actual or implied *ultimate* objectives. The future of social work will be clarified and its meaningfulness made apparent as this fact is recognized. Perhaps this would seem to contradict the previous statement that there can be no uniformity of ideology for social work either among social workers themselves or between religious and secular social work. On the contrary, though there may be sharp differences in strategy and in intent, fundamentally the objective is one. This fact is indicated in an address made by Robert H. MacCrae when he was director of the Community Chest of Detroit: "I believe that social work needs the church as much as the church needs social work. They need to understand each other. They are partners in a common enterprise of serving people. If organized religion were to disappear much of the social work would disappear in time because it would have lost its roots."[9]

We are not implying that the church or any denomination has a final or acceptable pattern for social welfare. We are contending, however, that the ultimate ends of social work and social welfare are fundamentally religious in nature. And only as the church comes to grips with this fact in a non-parochial manner will its own work be effective. Also, secular and public welfare will achieve its fullest realization only when it is motivated by this profound and basic understanding.

It can hardly be expected that all persons will accept a religious interpretation of life. However, all those who maintain and are sensitive to a religious faith, regardless of degree, start with the assumption that God is the primary

134

fact of life. Jews and Christians are in total agreement at this point. For all religious groups in America, therefore, there is the common ground of man's acknowledged dependence upon God as the source of life and the essence within which all life is lived. Christians assume that in the person of Jesus Christ, God entered into a very special relationship with man. In the person of Jesus Christ men see more vividly God's intentions for men and understand more clearly God's relationship to them.

Man's relationship to his fellow men in a life lived under God or in the totality of God's being is a different kind of life from one that makes no such requirements or has no such presuppositions. In Europe during the period of the church's most complete control, the church served as the determiner and final arbiter of God's society. Men learned at great cost that no institution is capable of interpreting accurately and adequately what God's order is. In America the Calvinist colonial life attempted to reconstruct a perfect order, and it was discovered again that men cannot dictate a type of life which ultimately can be lived only voluntarily. This continent is dotted with innumerable illustrations of present and past attempts to achieve the perfect society in small colonies or utopian communities: the Shaker communities, Amana, New Harmony, and many other communities attest to the eternal longing for the more perfect society which cares for its members. Largest of all, possibly, is the Mormon community, indigenous to America and avowing America as the New Jerusalem.

Each of the utopian and idealistic community experiments accepted the fundamental idea of God's sovereignty over all life. They sought to achieve in partial form and in limited geographic space what a fundamental religious philosophy requires.

It is, therefore, highly significant that all religious groups have sought the meaning of the term "community" as it comes into ever increasing prominence with scientific developments and the resulting increase in the proximity of men. Whether we will it or not, there is an integrity to society which biblical sources have been insisting upon for thousands of years but which in his parochialism man has resisted. Social welfare long ago partially discovered this. Religious leaders sensitive to social needs sought to quicken the life of the churches with this fact, as prophetic minds in all ages have attempted to do. Because the church as an institution is conservative (a characteristic of institutional life), it did not accept readily the radical interpretation of life that runs through the Hebrew-Christian record. It is no accident that many of the genuine religious prophets of our day have been very active in social work. Correspondingly, the most creative theologians of our times have been cognizant of and closely related to social welfare activities.

The concept of the community, therefore, which is basic to the Hebrew-Christian interpretation of life and which has been vividly brought into focus by the whole field of social welfare, has forced the more thoughtful and understanding people of this generation to recognize the religious foundations of society as a whole. This does not minimize the importance of individuals. It simply portrays them in their truer setting. Love toward individuals is not something apart from love in society. It is all of a piece. It is, indeed, only a person who can translate the idea of love—a genuine interest in and concern for one's fellow men, created by and in the likeness of God—into the situations which prevail in a highly organized technical society. Yet this is the task of religion and of the church in particular.

Social welfare is, then, the active outreach of love in society. Its effectiveness in re-creating society after God's intent will depend in the long run upon the measure of man's understanding of this fact and upon the degree of his dedication to it.

CHAPTER VIII

HEALTH

Medical science has advanced further in the past fifty years than in the two thousand years preceding this century. Since 1900 almost twenty years have been added to the life expectancy of Americans. Many diseases common but recently are today fast becoming extinct—malaria, tuberculosis, typhoid fever, smallpox, and others. At least this is true in America, and the skills that have eliminated these ailments are available for world application. However, in spite of these phenomenal gains, there are sharp differences of opinion among men in the medical profession itself and between a substantial percentage of doctors and representatives of other professions concerned for the total health of the nation. The controversy centers in the way in which these health resources shall be made available.

The Christian faith has no specific answer to the question. There is no Christian program of medicine. There is, however, a point of view from which a Christian medical practitioner or anyone concerned with health might regard a stewardship of medical science. It is from this perspective, therefore, that the problem of health and its availability is presented.

When the World Health Organization of the United Nations came into being, it defined health as "a state of complete physical, mental and social well-being and not merely the absence of disease or infirmity." It went on to add "the enjoyment of the highest attainable standard of health is one of the fundamental rights of every human being without distinction of race, religion, political belief, economic or social condition." Anthropologist Thomas Jesse Jones, citing some fundamental requirements for any kind of civilization, primitive or modern, says, "We conclude that physical welfare is the first essential of tribal life and probably of civilization as well."[1] In a similar vein, looking at the life of a modern political state, Benjamin Disraeli wrote, "The health of the people is really the foundation upon which all their happiness and all their powers as a state depend."[2]

America as a nation became intensely concerned about its health level during the great depression. Faced with the possibility of a decline in physical vitality and in the overall capacity of a nation to revive, we were willing to recognize that access to medical care was a basic minimum right, like food, clothing, and shelter.

Only a healthy nation is able to progress economically and morally. Significantly, the development programs in all the underdeveloped areas of the world have been posited on a program of health improvement. The possibilities for fulfilment of the life of an individual, a nation, or a community of nations depends upon health as a first imperative. One other piece of evidence can be added to the impressive accumulation—the National Safety Council's estimate that the loss to the national economy from accidents for a single year was $2,650 million.[3] The loss in productivity at a time when productivity is the determining factor in economic advance impairs the total national life. This, of course, leaves out what is to most of us the primary consideration—the personal disability, loss of income, impairment of personal resources, family burden, and all the rest.

The spiritual significance of health is not something apart from the other considerations of personal well-being, community safety, national stability, and international harmony. God as creator and sustainer of life is the being in whom health, welfare, and scientific progress is attained or falls short. Wholeness is the description of religious life. Health and wholeness have similar origins in language. But in many respects it is more difficult for a modern person to achieve wholeness or health than for a primitive tribesman

138

who is unconcerned about sanitation, television, clothing, etc. His life is less fractured psychologically. It becomes a more serious necessity for modern persons to grasp a sense of wholeness in the universe of One who is creator and sustainer. Modern man has had difficulty comprehending the full meaning of this religious truth. Current experience is forcing it upon him.

Realization of our inability to destroy our neighbor without destroying ourselves has been an eye-opening and a spiritually shaking experience. It has become apparent that no one part of the world can be secure and healthy with another part sick and insecure. The revelations of medical science concerning the interdependence of all men constitute one of the sources of God's revelation of his relationship to all nations and peoples. Jonah made a similar discovery some twenty-five hundred years ago.

DIFFERENCES OVER METHOD

But what of the relation of all this to the acrimonious contest between the American Medical Association and certain advocates of compulsory health insurance? Medical authorities, whether doctors or laymen responsible for the health of a community or nation, are in agreement that everyone should have access to medical care. It is a shadow upon the honor of this nation that there are still many persons for whom it is not available. Though rapid strides have been made in building hospitals and health centers and in sending medical personnel into otherwise unserved or inadequately served areas, we still suffer from a great deficiency.

The difference of opinion does not stem from disagreement as to whether health resources should be available. It stems rather from the method of paying for medical attention. Opposition to prepayment plans on the part of the majority of the American Medical Association has largely subsided. Lurid history was made with the pressure exerted by the predominant medical group to stop such ventures as the Elk City, Oklahoma, Cooperative Health Program and Hospital, sponsored by the Farmers' Union, and the Group Health Association in Washington, D.C. These and other issues had to be resolved by legislative action and a Supreme Court decision. Similarly, there was vehement resistance to various voluntary insurance plans, such as Blue Cross and Blue Shield, now accepted and welcomed as the alternative to a compulsory medical insurance program. The New York Academy of Medicine in 1946 heartily indorsed voluntary prepayment plans and the National Health Assembly in 1948 commended them for offering to their members the best of medical care. They were, according to the assembly, the best means then available for improving the distribution of medical care and were to be encouraged by every possible means.[4]

Now that voluntary health insurance has become an accepted fact and is given the approval of the established medical organization, it is necessary to look at its adequacy and to consider further resources.

The Social Security Act of 1935 constitutes a watershed in American social history. With its enactment it was recognized that the costs of welfare must be distributed. Since 1935 federal and state security and welfare legislation has come in a steady flow—old age pensions, unemployment insurance, aid to dependent children, hospital construction. In addition, there has come into the labor-management picture a large element of health and welfare benefits frequently described as "fringe benefits."

We as a nation have accepted the fact that the financial burden of illness falls unevenly on the population. Health is no longer a luxury. It is an integral part of a nation's total policy. This fact cannot be obscured by slogans or name-calling, however clever or seemingly convincing.

140

PUBLIC RESOURCES

Developments in medical practice have made corresponding changes in the methods of applying these new resources. We take for granted the elimination of diseases common a generation ago but may be unaware that the attack upon them was made possible by new approaches to the whole problem of medical practice. For instance, in addition to the highly correlated research work of hospitals and university training centers, the largest center of medical research in the world is conducted by the federal government with the combined resources of the army and navy. With twenty million veterans eligible for medical assistance, veterans hospitals have been constructed as teaching institutions close to big universities and have made possible greater variety in medical experience. They have put at the disposal of the medical practice resources otherwise less easily attainable.

It is interesting, too, that half the total treatment given to veterans is for mental disturbance. With the great shortage of psychiatrists and specialists in mental cases, it is only under government auspices that adequate attention to this field can be given, at least for the time being. The state and federal governments have assumed responsibility for care of mental illness. At the time of this writing 97 per cent of all beds in mental institutions are financed by government agencies.

Another change that has taken place in the general attitude toward sickness lies in the area of rehabilitation. Whereas formerly many injured and disabled persons were allowed to disintegrate with no expectation of return to any kind of usefulness, the great strides in rehabilitation under state and federal auspices have restored hope and self-sufficiency to many. But, aside from the tremendous social gains from converting physically disabled people into self-sustaining citizens, the economic values have been very great. In 1947, for example, the Office of Vocational Rehabilitation restored the working ability of about 44,000 persons. In 1951 these people were earning more than $70 million and paid to the federal government $5 million in income taxes.[5]

It is those at the lower end of the economic scale who, because of inadequate diet and insufficient care generally, may need the largest amount of medical assistance. Yet by virtue of their economic state they are unable to provide this for themselves. In keeping with the theory that health is indivisible for a nation, the public health resources and agencies have provided assistance. This generally consists of treatment for venereal disease and tuberculosis, of child care, and also of dental and orthopedic attention. Expectant mothers may also receive aid. More recently the service provided by clinics for the needy has begun to include treatment of cancer and heart disease and care for mental hygiene needs. The Rockefeller Foundation, which began its work in 1909, has had a distinguished record of meeting the health needs of many parts of the world. It has brought its vast resources to bear on the task of aiding governments in the solution of their health problems. Among policies and principles early adopted was one holding that "public health is a function of government and that long range results can be accomplished only by building up national and local health administrations to carry on in the future."

Thus the story goes on. History is being made so rapidly that no account of federal participation in the health program of the nation can be complete or final. Mention should be made, however, of the Hill-Burton Bill, which made possible the expenditure of approximately $150 million annually through 1955 for the construction of community hospitals, with special assistance to the rural areas where such medical care was not available before.

NON-GOVERNMENTAL PROGRAMS

Because of their widespread adoption across the nation, Blue Cross and Blue Shield are household words. They are insurance plans rather than instruments for the development of medical practice. Nevertheless, they have substantially influenced the development of uniform practices within hospitals. In general these hospital insurance plans covering medical and surgical attention are designed to share the risk and reduce the heavy expenses for which most persons rarely have adequate reserve.

Into the field of health insurance various segments of the labor movement have been steadily moving. The International Ladies Garment Workers' Union and the Amalgamated Clothing Workers' Union have set up, through collective bargaining, employer-financed programs. The United Mine Workers' Union, through collective bargaining, has put into force a medical care program for its members. Almost daily new contracts are being negotiated with industrial organizations in which medical provisions are included. The auto workers and the steel workers have been in the forefront of this movement. The Steel Industry Board in 1949 issued a statement that pretty generally reflects the point of view of a large segment of the nation. In the absence of adequate government programs, it said, all industry owes its workers provision for maintenance of the human body in the form of medical benefits and provision for depreciation in the form of old age retirement funds. Like the maintenance and depreciation of plant and machinery, the cost of these provisions should be considered "one of the fixed costs of doing business—one of the first charges before profits."[6]

The types and extent of various health programs are too numerous for documentation. More should be said, however, about the prepayment type of plan. This requires the payment of a stated sum, either annually or monthly, for which the patient secures a stipulated variety of health services. Among the best known hospitals conducting these plans are Trinity Hospital in Little Rock, Arkansas; the Ross Loos Clinic in Los Angeles; the Perminente Hospital in Oakland, California; the Elk City Community Hospital Clinic in Oklahoma; and the Health Cooperative of Puget Sound in Seattle, Washington.[7]

The purpose in mentioning a few of the health plans in these paragraphs is to indicate not only the numerous agencies that have come into being but also the great variety in the type of protection they offer.

GROUP PRACTICE

Men graduating from medical school have been increasingly desirous of affiliating themselves with a company of doctors with broader total interests and more inclusive services than are possible in a single man's practice. The high degree of specialization which has emerged in the medical profession makes it impossible for any single man to prepare for all situations with which he might be confronted. The family-doctor type of relationship so honored in American community life has necessarily been modified. Advantages of group service, in addition to the broader resources of specialization, include mutual stimulus and professional advancement, less confinement, and an equalizing of economic opportunity. The reputation of the entire group or clinic supports the practitioner, and the burden for sustaining a practice is not placed upon a single individual. In some instances the group-practice arrangement has been developed in connection with prepayment or insurance plans. Resistance has been expressed to such innovations, principally on the ground that this destroys the relationship between the doctor and the patient and introduces an element of coercion, reducing the patient's selection and free choice of doctor. Gradually, however, the resistance to such plans seems to be disappearing in the light of the greater efficiency and the satisfaction both to patient and practitioner.

GAINS AND DEFICIENCIES

The fact that the life span of the average American has increased twenty years in the last fifty is, of course, cause for gratification. At the same time, along with the improvement in health statistics related to longevity, there is the increase in diseases that affect older persons—heart ailments, cancer, etc.

Nevertheless, the greatest loss and highest percentage of debility is among those of low-income and minority status. The life expectancy of the non-white minority population is shorter than that of the white majority by 8.68 years—a disparity which has been reduced from 15 years in the past half-century. Nevertheless, a disparity which exists solely because of race is a reflection and blot upon our national life.

The Negro population constitutes approximately 10 per cent of the total population, but only 1.8 per cent of the total number of physicians are Negroes.[8] Inadequate opportunities for the training of Negro physicians and dentists is largely responsible for this condition. The unwillingness of medical schools to accept Negro students for training is not solely due to race; the inadequate preparation Negroes have had is also responsible. This, of course, goes back to the lack of opportunities for training at the elementary, secondary, and college levels. The action of the Supreme Court in insisting that the same opportunity shall be accorded to all groups can be expected to have profound implications for the training of minority professional leadership. "In the South there is one Negro doctor to 4,908 patients on the average, and in Mississippi the ratio is one to 18,527. Only ten of the 105 Negro specialists are located in the South, exclusive of the District of Columbia, and 26 (30%) are in one city, Washington."[9]

But not all the deficiency in health resources is among minorities. A 1948 report to the President on the nation's health said that routine medical care was beyond the means of half the families in the United States, those with incomes of $3,000 or less. Another 30 per cent, with incomes between $3,000 and $5,000, would have to make great sacrifices or go into debt to pay for severe or chronic illness.[10]

Tied in with the patient's ability to pay is the availability of doctors. According to one survey, there is one physician for 1,431 people in South Carolina and one for 571 people in California. In Mississippi there is one dentist for 5,263 people while in Oregon there is one for 990. There is one hospital bed for 749 persons in South Carolina and one for 154 in Wisconsin. The reason is that South Carolina and Mississippi are relatively poor states, while California, Oregon, and Wisconsin are relatively rich. It is not surprising that doctors and dentists want to practice where they may be well paid for their work.[11]

CHRISTIAN FAITH AND MEETING
HEALTH NEEDS

The Apostle Paul designated the whole human being as the temple of God: "Do you know that you are God's temple and that God's Spirit makes its home in you? If anyone destroys the temple of God, God will destroy him. For the temple of God is sacred, and that is what you are" (I Cor. 3:16–17).

We are, truly, the house in which God lives even as we live in him. Here is the inseparable tie of man with all the rest of creation. Man, thus, is a part of God's being and God is in man—a fact of infinite significance for human life.

146

Modern medicine is illustrating in ways heretofore un-
realized the degree of unity present in all life and in the
whole of human society. Pellagra or rickets in an American
sharecropper or the yaws in a Malay States child, we now
know, has repercussions on the welfare of people everywhere. Loss in vitality of one person means reduction in
the vitality of the entire community, not to mention the
consequences of communicable diseases.

All health is public health. We are being forcibly confronted with the full meaning of the biblical insistence that
all men are brothers. The integrity of society is a spiritual
concept. For many of us, presumably, our training has been
limited and individualistic. The profound wisdom of the
Hebrew-Christian understanding of society has, therefore,
been only slightly comprehended. Now the developments
of science have served to convey to the twentieth-century
man a depth of wisdom he could not grasp in the literature
of his faith. The team of the researcher and the medical
practitioner have become, consciously or unconsciously, the
convincing exponents of religious truth. He who would preserve and restore health is a minister in the fullest sense of
the word. He may truly be a Christ to his neighbor.

The doctor's position today is such that he must be
more than technically competent. He must be an informed,
cultured person commanding the respect of leaders in every
phase of human activity. He must be a highly educated
citizen "sharing responsibility with other community leaders for the creation of those conditions that will improve
the general economic and social well-being and thus the
positive health of the people as a whole."[12]

The preparation of medical personnel qualified according
to the foregoing description will probably not result solely
from the medical profession's own intentions. A broadly
informed public will encourage such a quality of professional leadership. The chief purpose of such a chapter as

this, dealing as it attempts to do with Christianity and the meeting of health needs, is to help sensitize Christian people to the relation between spiritual life and health resources. It is understandable that a profession so intimately related to the experiences of life and death should be religiously sensitive. It remains now for informed and concerned Christians both within and without the medical profession to help devise and encourage a health policy commensurate with our resources and demonstrating the compassion of Christ.

Until now the planning of a health policy has frequently been clouded by name-calling. The medical profession is rightfully jealous of its standards and highly selective of its membership. Many of its members are hostile toward plans which made low-cost medical service available, ostensibly because the doctor-patient relation would be injured or standards would be lowered. The public suspects that the opposition is often for less idealistic reasons, despite all that the public relations firms can do.

At the same time it may well be that those pressing for greater availability and lower costs of medical resources are also motivated by purposes less than idealistic. Political considerations or excess enthusiasm may enter their reasoning.

We have been contending that both economic and political considerations are basically spiritual. Members of the medical profession and all those most deeply concerned for the well-being of others will serve their fellow men even more fully as they deal with this issue in its spiritual dimensions.

CHAPTER IX

CHURCH AND STATE

As these lines are being read it is almost a certainty that in some state or federal court a case is being heard involving the principle of church-state separation. It is equally certain that one or more of these cases will be appealed to the United States Supreme Court, so many cases having already been tried with important issues yet unresolved. The church-state issue is subject to almost continuous reinterpretation.

INTRODUCTION

Americans pride themselves on their tolerance and on the far-sightedness of their nation's founders in assuring the right to differing points of view. Nevertheless, there are major decisions confronting the American people which, even if resolved after the pattern established by the Founding Fathers, are fraught with friction. They will at least temporarily disrupt our harmony.

Even in the comparatively short life of this nation it is apparent that the wisdom of those who sought the separation of church and state was fundamentally sound. Almost a century and a half of experience has justified the original reasons for insisting that the church and the state shall not interfere with each other. Where the church has sought domination, the freedom to develop a nation's life has been curtailed. Where governments have sought to dictate religious life, a suppression of the finest human qualities has ensued.

After long deliberation and a review of many proposals, there was written into the Constitution as a part of the First Amendment the sentence which helped make this nation different from any other in history: "Congress shall make no law respecting an establishment of religion or

149

prohibiting the free exercise thereof." It is around this sentence and its implications that policy decisions determining the life of this nation have been and will continue to be made. Because major decisions involving the interpretation of that sentence must now be made, we include it in the category of those concerns which confront all thoughtful Christians.

SOURCE OF THE AMERICAN CHURCH-STATE POLICY

The authors of the Constitution had witnessed the consequences of an established church. They had abundant evidence from the life of their own times in Europe to know what tragic consequences ensue from a church-dominated state or a state-dominated church. Here in this new land, with an opportunity to make a fresh start free of the shackles of a religious institution, it was possible for religion to find its normal expression as men related themselves to their Creator without official interference. The authors of the Constitution knew that even religious institutions tend to try to gain privileges for themselves. Thus they inhibit the development of new and constructive ideas. This awareness that religious institutions in general and churches in particular must constantly be watched lest they inhibit new ideas and possibilities for truth is an integral part of Protestantism. Protestantism encourages the constant search for new truth, even though it may go contrary to institutions created to support a particular set of religious ideas. In this sense the authors of the Constitution were unconsciously, but nevertheless effectively, implementing a basic Protestant conviction.

Thus it came about that no single institution or religious conviction was to be favored. This new land, it was hoped, would be spared the agonizing conflicts which had sapped the vitality of the Old World and held it in bonds.

150

All seekers for truth and all supporters of any religious ideas were to have complete freedom to make their own way in proportion as their ideas and convictions gained support. In the same process government would be free to exercise itself and to be the subject of experiments. Government, thus, could itself serve the whole people and accomplish the ends for which government exists.

No other nation in history had been thus conceived. In other nations religious organizations had been either the tools or the masters of government. Ultimately, both religion and government had suffered. The authors of the Constitution were close enough to some of these restraining and corrosive experiences to know their baneful consequences. Thus, if possible, they were determined that this new nation should be unencumbered.

Also, because the authors of the Constitution had a deep sense of the importance of religion, they were determined to preserve their government from its distortions. The evidence of their religious interest is voluminous and conclusive both in their personal lives and in their writings. Their determination to keep personal religious preference out of the document of the Constitution attests all the more to their qualities of personal greatness.

Those living in the twentieth century have had abundant opportunity to observe the tragic consequences of church-state integration. They can be eternally grateful, therefore, that church-state separation has been assured to our country. This does not carry with it automatic guaranties. In our time the theory of church-state separation has been challenged and distorted—witness the capitulation of some Protestant and Catholic leaders to Hitler and naziism and the concordat between Mussolini and the Vatican. In Spain the close tie between Franco and the church has carried with it consequences destructive both to personal liberty and to the well-being of the nation.

Before reviewing some of the situations with which our own nation is confronted, it is appropriate to review instances in history when church-state separation either did not exist or collapsed.

The Hebrew theocracy came into being because of a solemn conviction that all life must be subject to God. Rulers were chosen because of their depth of dedication. What happened to them after election or choice as political leaders constitutes one of the revelations in Old Testament history. Political power reinforced by religious authority is quickly prostituted. Genuine religion had to be brought to the fore by prophets who challenged political power and its abuse. The role of the priests serving the ruling political authorities is symbolized by the story of Micaiah. Because the Bible was so large a part of the education of the Founding Fathers, it is reasonable to expect that they knew this story and the many others of Old Testament history.

The power of the Christian movement in the Roman Empire was such that not even the most powerful political and military ruler in the world at the time could subject it. Constantine practiced a policy which politicians have always found expedient. Its modern slang expression is "if you can't beat 'em, join 'em." Constantine saw that his empire needed the cohesiveness and vitality that the Christian faith provided for its adherents. It involved no conversion on the emperor's part. It did open the door for Christian expansion in the empire, but at the price of collusion with the state. Men aware of history, such as Thomas Jefferson, Benjamin Franklin, James Madison, George Mason, John Adams, Patrick Henry, Daniel Carroll, John Witherspoon, Isaac Backus, and others, were presumably acquainted with this story, too.

In the visual-image album of many of us is the picture of Henry IV standing in the cold outside the door of Hilde-

brand (Pope Gregory VII) begging forgiveness for having
defied the Pope's authority. Hildebrand excommunicated
Henry and, in spite of the latter's defiance, Henry came
humbly asking forgiveness. This did not end the contest,
however. Henry finally drove Hildebrand from the papacy
and set up one of his own choosing.

The history of the contests between religious leaders and
state authorities in England is filled with fireworks and is a
blight upon both the religious and the political life of that
nation. One of its consequences was the departure of the
"Mayflower" filled with persons seeking freedom from the
turmoil and restrictions of a land torn by the church-state
controversy. It was they who could state:

In the name of God, Amen. We, whose names are under-
written . . . having undertaken for the glory of God and advancement of the Christian faith and honor of our king and
country, a voyage to plant the first colony in the northern parts
of Virginia; do, by these presence, solemnly and mutually in
the presence of God and one another covenant and combine
ourselves together into a civil body politic for our better ordering and preservation and furtherance of the ends aforesaid; and
by virtue hereof do enact, constitute and frame, such just and
equal laws, ordinances, acts, constitutions and offices from time
to time as shall be thought most meet and convenient for the
general good of the colony; under which we promise all due
submission and obedience. . . .

Thus, out of the church-state contest in England arose the
Mayflower Compact, one of the most important documents of history.

In Europe, where kingships were precarious, the power
of religion was necessary to bolster corrupt and venal institutions. Even Augustine and Aquinas, temperate and godly
men, could give sanction to the brutalities of the Inquisition. Though the church in its fullest sense is God's instru-

ment on earth, it is also administered by mortal men subject to very human desires.

Even the Reformation, which began as a defiance of conformity to an institution and of rigid demands for religious observance, was not itself free from insistence upon conformity. Luther and Calvin, the most prominent men in the history of the Reformation, in their eagerness for man's freedom could not resist the temptation to dictate the nature of that freedom, using political instruments.

In England, under the leadership of Cromwell, the dominant religious patterns of the time allowed no place for Roman Catholics. Great causes conducted in the name of freedom can be corrupted.

When, on American soil, freedom-seeking people set up a new way of life and a colony whose purpose it was to illustrate and demonstrate the godly community, only a short time passed before the Plymouth colonists prescribed orthodoxy and forbade deviation. The result was the establishment of still another colony under the intellectual and spiritual leadership of Roger Williams.

The story is long and unvarying and, when unfolded in its fulness, makes for sober thought. It is, therefore, a source of deep satisfaction that the men who were intrusted with the founding of a new nation had the courage to act upon their knowledge of the injury done where church and state were too closely intertwined and thus saved their descendants from some of the fate of other nations. They established the principle that the relations between a man and his Creator were his private concern.

Not only the sad story of church-state relations in other lands but also the existence of an established church in five American colonies caused the Constitution-makers to reject this arrangement for the new nation. Political considerations were also significant. In fact, a number of interdependent factors are responsible for the American experiment. Among these the most important were probably the English Act of Toleration in 1689, the multiplicity of sects in the American colonies, the fact that many Americans were without church affiliation, the rise of trade and commerce, the exigencies of the Revolutionary War, the success of Roger Williams' and William Penn's experiments, the writings of Locke, and the influence of the social contract theory, of rationalism, and of deism.[1]

In Massachusetts and Connecticut vigorous support for the Revolution had been provided by the pastors and laymen of the established church, the Congregational. But, as Anson Phelps Stokes points out, the leadership in securing religious freedom as finally incorporated in the Constitution came less from these established state churches than from others that either had not been accorded the status of establishment or had been removed from that status. The Episcopal church had been the established church of Virginia. Subject to the crown, it had not provided leadership in the Revolution proportionate to that of other denominations. This is understandable. However, when, after the Revolution, an attempt was made to accord to this particular church a special status, there arose vehement protest and effective opposition from lay members who had participated in the Revolution, namely, Madison, Mason, and, possibly most important, Jefferson. When attempt was made to incorporate the Protestant Episcopal church in Virginia, giving title of the churches to the ministers and providing special favors for them, there was prepared the "memorial and remonstrance against religious assessments" containing fifteen arguments against the bill.

This attempt to establish the Episcopal church in Virginia failed. Presently the establishment of churches in other states was relinquished also: in Connecticut in 1817 and in Massachusetts in 1833. Stokes points out significantly that the two established churches have been the slowest to expand in America.[2]

It is interesting that among the early attempts to formulate what is now the First Amendment the word "denomination" was used. When the final action was taken, however, the word "denomination" did not appear. The authors of the American Magna Carta, our Bill of Rights, wanted no confusion in this matter. They intended that the import of the First Amendment should apply broadly and inclusively. They wished to do more than simply prevent any one denomination from having the advantage in relation to the state.[3] They voted down the reference to denomination.

The first ten Amendments became a part of the Constitution on the ratification of Virginia in December, 1791. The Fourteenth Amendment was adopted in 1868:

> No State shall make or enforce any law which shall abridge the privileges or immunities of citizens of the United States; nor shall any State deprive any person of life, liberty, or property without due process of law; nor deny to any person within its jurisdiction the equal protection of the laws.

The Fourteenth Amendment is linked with the First Amendment in that it seeks to protect in the legislation and the conduct of the several states those rights and liberties protected in the First Amendment. Religious freedom and immunity from a national establishment of religion, having been guaranteed in the First Amendment, are, in the opinion of some members of the Supreme Court at least, provided protection against possible encroachment by the states.

Such a brief condensation cannot begin to do justice to the rich historical soil out of which came church-state separation in this nation. One conclusion is inescapable,

156

however: the total weight of the forces working to create a
new nation called for a pattern of church-state relationship
unlike anything prevailing in the Old World. New winds
of freedom and new awareness of the dignity of man as a
child of God called for new modes of political expression.
Only thus could this fresh approach to man's political and
social needs be given expression.

But as was indicated in the opening paragraphs of this
chapter, the separation of church and state could not be
guaranteed automatically simply because provision had
been made for it in the very first amendment.

That the United States came into being in an atmosphere friendly and encouraging to religious expression is almost so apparent that to repeat it is superfluous. Nevertheless, there are those who feel that, unless explicit avowal of
our belief in God is included in such primary documents
as the Constitution, it may be doubted. Hence, to this day
there are those who seek to insert in official documents and
proclamations some reference to the Deity, presumably on
the assumption that this would affirm our religious interest
as a nation. In 1954 the Pledge of Allegiance was altered
to include the phrase "under God." It would seem that the
innumerable evidences of consideration for religion, such
as tax exemption to religious organizations, chaplaincy in
the armed forces, and prayers at the opening of each session
of Congress, would attest to the absence of hostility toward
religion if not to a fervent espousal thereof.

But it is precisely at the points of difference of opinion
as to the ways in which government shall foster particular
religious agencies or movements that the First Amendment
has had to be brought into operation. We turn, therefore,
to some of the present-day situations involving the principle espoused from our nation's beginnings.

RECENT ISSUES INVOLV-
ING SEPARATION

Early in the nation's life the question of the right of clergymen to serve the government as public officials was settled. There had been attempts to bar clergymen from public office. When Thomas Jefferson proposed this restriction on ministerial officeholding, Madison asked: "Does not the exclusion of ministers of the Gospel as such violate a fundamental principle of liberty by punishing a religious profession with a deprivation of his civil right?" Jefferson later agreed.[4]

During the period when the Mormons were establishing themselves as a cohesive and vigorous denomination, the practice of polygamy was sanctioned and encouraged by the leaders of this church. A need for additional population in the new Promised Land of the West to which they had migrated and a desire to increase the potential leadership of the colony combined to foster the practice of polygamy. Into this situation it was necessary for the federal government to enter. An act of Congress forbade bigamy. In 1878 and again in 1890 a Supreme Court ruled that polygamy and bigamy were crimes despite their religious sanction. In 1890 the Church of Jesus Christ of Latter Day Saints yielded to the federal law.

It is a universal human desire to want other people to be like ourselves. In every society a premium is placed upon conformity. There is no reason to expect that American life would be any different in this respect. Nor is it. The non-conformist, therefore, is almost always looked upon with suspicion. In this regard religion has extraordinary consequences. On the one hand, it is an instrument making for conformity. On the other hand, in its prophetic forms and variations it encourages non-conformity.

Because religion has been so useful in helping to achieve conformity in national life, governments have eagerly sought its assistance. Correspondingly, they have suppressed non-conformity or any attempt to express a variation in religious conduct. The whole history of state-church interdependence and mutual support stems from this extraordinary characteristic of religious life. Religious institutions gladly accept the aid of the state if it helps to suppress radical or varying forms of religious life. This was the situation behind the Inquisition and behind the holy experiments in communal religious life in Geneva, in England, in Massachusetts, and in other parts of America. Patriotism and religion in the minds of many persons are synonymous.

Fortunately for the life of this nation, they were not synonymous to the authors of the Constitution and of the Bill of Rights in particular. These men knew that religious freedom carried with it the right to differ from the standard pattern of citizen conduct even if it meant rejection of what most people thought to be patriotism. Our nation has recognized the rights of conscientious objectors to pursue the requirements of their faith and conscience. We have never been quite sure what constitutes a conscientious objector and our national policy has varied. Nevertheless, there is ingrained in our national fabric the recognition of men's rights to refuse to bear arms if their religions teaches them otherwise.

A religious movement known as Jehovah's Witnesses has presented the United States with one of its more dramatic illustrations of church-state separation. Jehovah's Witnesses refuse to salute the American flag on the ground that their loyalties are to a Supreme Deity and to salute the flag would be to imply that there was some other entity higher than God. In the Ten Commandments it is stipulated, "You must have no other gods beside me." Other religious

159

groups, notably in England, have refused to remove their hats in the presence of civil authorities for the same reason.

The children of a Jehovah's Witness named Walter Gobitis were expelled from the schools of Minersville, Pennsylvania, for refusing to participate in the flag salute required of all school children. The case went to the Supreme Court. A lower court had held "that a ceremonial device to instill respect for country did not out-weigh the freedom of religious conscience."[5] In a first decision the Supreme Court, with one dissenting voice, reversed the decision of the lower courts and insisted that, in the interest of national unity, the flag salute should be required. Such a wave of opposition to the decision swept over the country that the Court, in 1943, reversed its decision, with a number of justices who had voted in the affirmative on the previous case acknowledging that they were in error.

Because the Jehovah's Witnesses' organization has been involved in so many suits, many of them contesting their right to present their particular points of view either on the street or at the door of homes to which they seek admission in order to propagandize their faith, it is appropriate to include here one other case which established their and our freedom to present religious beliefs.

Members of that body had attempted to sell religious literature on the streets of New Haven. In the literature there were severe condemnations of Roman Catholicism as well as a presentation of other matters of their faith. A New Haven ordinance forbade solicitation of money or subscriptions for religious, charitable, or philanthropic causes unless approved by the secretary of the Public Welfare Council. Newton Cantwell and his two sons, who were doing the soliciting, were convicted by the Court of Common Pleas of New Haven County. The case was carried to the Supreme Court, which decided that the act under which the Cantwells were convicted was unconstitutional since it denied religious freedom. The case has additional significance in the fact that the Court held the Fourteenth Amendment applicable to religious guaranties of the Bill of Rights. It indicated, therefore, that the federal government was prepared to protect religious freedom in the courts of the states.

Justice Owen Roberts, in delivering the opinion of the Court, stated:

The appellants urged that to require them to obtain a certificate as a condition of soliciting support for their views amounts to a prior restraint on the exercise of their religion within the meaning of the Constitution. . . . Such a censorship of religion as the means of determining its right to survive is a denial of liberty protected by the First Amendment and included in the liberty which is within the protection of the Fourteenth.[6]

Local communities and states increasingly have had to turn to the federal government for funds to provide welfare services. This necessity has highlighted issues of the allocation of federal funds for denominational welfare services. Symptomatic, perhaps, of all such federal appropriations is the Hill-Burton Act originally passed in 1946, known as the Hospital Survey and Construction Act. More than 80 per cent[7] of the funds allocated to denominational hospitals have gone to Roman Catholic hospitals, and Protestant and Jewish hospitals have also received benefits from the Hill-Burton Act. The conviction against the allocation of money for hospitals is less clear than that against aid for parochial education under the various denominations. State courts have ruled favorably on the appropriation of these funds on the ground that people are not likely to be converted in the short time they are in hospitals. The issue came to very special consideration, however, when a Roman Catholic hospital in Poughkeepsie, New York, demanded that seven physicians "sever their connections with the Planned Parenthood Association or be barred from entry into the hospital."[8] The hospital had received substantial funds under the Hill-Burton Act. Surely it must become increasingly apparent that a hospital which accepts tax money from all the people can hardly bar those who may happen to differ in a principle of religious belief. The Poughkeepsie hospital case with its far-reaching implications has yet to come before the Supreme Court.

Sporadic attempts have been made throughout the history of this nation to make certain that tax money shall not be channeled through denominational organizations for distribution in welfare situations. In some states it is possible to distribute tax funds through denominational welfare agencies. The assumption is that a basic need is being met rather than that a particular denomination is being aided. In other states the state constitution forbids allocation of any public money or property to a sect, church denomination, etc. The absence of uniformity and the fact that obviously certain denominations are deriving special benefits from tax funds will bring this situation to wider public knowledge and presumably to the Supreme Court.

The most dramatic and most highly publicized of all federal tax allocations for welfare purposes is, of course, the issue that comes to the fore in every session of Congress—federal aid to education. It is commonly understood that one of the two major obstacles to equalizing educational opportunities throughout the nation is the insistence on the part of churches, particularly of the Roman Catholic church, that federal funds shall be available for parochial schools as well as for public schools. The other basis of opposition has come from those who insist that states now providing separate educational facilities to Negro and white children shall not be compelled to offer equal opportunities to all youth.

A substantial bloc of congressmen has contended that federal aid to education shall not include assistance to parochial schools. At the time of this writing, any attempts to provide federal aid to education that do not give assistance to parochial schools and insist upon equal educational opportunities have met with opposition from the Roman Catholic church and from certain southern representatives. Compromises have been attempted, notably the Taft-Thomas compromise permitting federal funds to be used "only for such schools as the Constitution or statutes of the several states make eligible for state support." This attempt to provide a concession to parochial schools was met by vigorous Protestant opposition.

Among the arguments for federal aid to parochial education is that which says that parochial schools already save the taxpayers a large sum of money. It is also suggested that Roman Catholic parents sending their children to parochial schools are taxed twice (there are other than Catholic parochial schools, of course, but similar complaints do not come from parents sending children to those schools). The American theory of separation of church and state would insist that parents of parochial school children have every right to have their children educated in parochial schools so long as the standards are acceptable to state departments of education. This question was settled in the famous Oregon case (1925). But the fact remains that the purpose of parochial education is primarily to keep children in contact with their church. If parents wish to have their children thus trained, this is their privilege, but they should also expect to meet the additional costs thereof.

The Protestant who chooses to send his children either to a public school or to a private church school or to some other private school may not assume that the burden of religious education is to be borne by the school. But nei ther does he regard the public school as a solely secular or godless institution. In itself, he believes, it contributes to the total religious life of the pupil. Protestantism acknowledges that the growth of the pupil is integral to his religious development, which does not take place only in a church but is as truly found in the educative process in the public school. Basically, the public school is not a secular institution—it has profound religious implications.

The contest for funds to support parochial schools becomes, thus, a sectarian issue—not a question of the religiousness or the absence of religion in the public school itself. It is to the question of the teaching of particular religious doctrines or points of view in the public school or in time allotted for public school activities that we turn next.

Decisions of the Supreme Court in three cases involving religious education in the public schools have made judicial history in America and necessitated major readjustments in many communities. As a result of these three decisions one thing is very certain: still other decisions will be forthcoming.

The three cases are as follows:

The Everson case (1947).—A taxpayer challenged the right of a Board of Education to reimburse parents of parochial school students who used local transportation to attend parochial schools. The United States Supreme Court in a 5 to 4 decision upheld the constitutionality of the law passed by the New Jersey legislature which permits such reimbursement. The Supreme Court held that "the state may validly enact legislation to protect all children from the hazards of traffic; and . . . since the state may validly enact legislation to provide children with a secular education it may validly enact legislation to transport children to a place where others than the state supply that secular education."[9]

Since there are many states providing the same facilities and assistance, the action was, of course, of wide importance. Of great importance, also, was the fact that in this case the Court held that "in the words of Jefferson, the clause against establishment of religion by law was intended to erect 'a wall of separation between church and state.'" The use of the phrase "a wall of separation between church and state" has become a symbol in the church-state controversy.

The McCollum case (1948).—School children in Champaign, Illinois, were permitted to participate in religious education classes for one period each week. If a majority of the pupils in each class elected to participate in the religious education program they might remain in their classroom; other children could go elsewhere during that time. The son of Mrs. Vashti McCollum was the only pupil in his room who did not participate, as his family did not approve of the nature of the religious education program. The Illinois Supreme Court had upheld the constitutionality of the Champaign program. When the case came to the United States Supreme Court, that Court held that religious education conducted in a school building constituted an assistance to a particular religion. It could hardly have done otherwise, having insisted in the Everson case that there was "a wall between church and state." The effect of the McCollum decision was to remove released-time religious education programs from school buildings. As Justice Black wrote, "This is beyond all question a utilization of the tax-established and tax-supported public school system to aid religious groups to spread their faiths. And it falls squarely under the ban of the First Amendment (made applicable to the states by the Fourteenth) as we interpreted it in Everson vs. Board of Education."[10] But the McCollum case still left undecided the question of the issue of time being taken from the school day for purposes of religious education. That was to come next.

The Zorach case (1952).—A Protestant family named Zorach and a Jewish family named Gluck brought suit challenging the New York State program of released-time religious education in which children went from public school during the last hour of the school day to the place of religious instruction in the building of their particular faith. The Supreme Court upheld the constitutionality of the New York released-time program on the assumption that the school does no more than close its doors—or suspend its operations—to those who want to repair to their religious sanctuary for religious instruction. As Leo Pfeffer contends, "This means releasing children for religious instruction and not releasing those who do not want to partake of religious instruction."[11]

VATICAN APPOINTMENT

More sensational and perhaps charged with more heat than any of the issues cited above is the question of an ambassador to the Vatican. In 1939 President Roosevelt invited Dr. George A. Buttrick, president of the Federal Council of Churches of Christ in the U.S.A., and Dr. Cyrus Adler, president of the Jewish Theological Seminary, to act as his advisers in matters relating to their particular faiths. At the same time he appointed Myron C. Taylor his "personal representative" to His Holiness, Pope Pius XII. The Protestant and Jewish "advisers," as well as the rest of the nation, shortly realized that their positions were hardly of equal status. The President's appointment of a personal representative was quickly recognized as at least a semiofficial relationship between this nation and the Vatican, a status suspected by a very large percentage of the nation. On few issues has Protestantism been so thoroughly united. Despite protests the appointment stood. Myron

C. Taylor resigned in 1950 and a successor was not appointed.

In 1951 President Truman submitted to the Senate the name of General Mark W. Clark for confirmation as a full-fledged ambassador to the Vatican. Opposition to this appointment was almost unanimous among Protestants. General Clark finally withdrew his name, and no other person was nominated.

Arguments pro and con regarding the appointment are voluminous. Possibly the most telling one is the insistence that the appointment is inconsistent with the American principle of separation of church and state. Many arguments along the lines of expediency, history, and analogy with other nations and their relation to the church are of secondary importance. The fact is that such an appointment would give a special privilege and recognition to a particular denomination. The appointment would, without question, be to a religious organization and not to a political state.

The furor caused by the appointment of the personal representative and the attempted appointment of an ambassador to the Vatican only proved again that deep in the American way of life is a conviction that no single denomination or religious group shall be accorded special privileges.

The church-state issues that have been mentioned constitute but a small fraction of many such issues. They are cited to indicate that not only is the subject widespread in its implications but it is continually before us.

CRITERIA FOR CHRISTIANS

The fact that the authors of the Constitution were determined to perpetuate the separation of church and state in this nation is in itself hardly a sufficient reason for future generations to be bound thereby. Times and conditions change. Nevertheless, the reasons which underlay the decision of the Constitution's authors are no less valid today than in 1789.

The human desires for the advancement of institutions and the attainment of conformity are as present in modern society as in any previous period. Though each generation feels it might evade the catastrophes befalling preceding generations, any reading of history points to the fact that people are rarely wise enough to avoid the pitfalls of their ancestors unless restrictions are set up for them, either by themselves or by others. This, at least, is what the authors of the Constitution did for the generations that followed them. As a result, this nation has been singularly free of ecclesiastical manipulation in its government. This is not to say that we have not had such influence in government. Actually, there has been a great deal of it. It has been kept within the bounds we know, however, largely because this prescription was written into the very structure of our nation.

Legislative and constitutional prohibitions against church interference in government does not prohibit the influence of religion in the life of the nation as a whole. It is apparent from the records of early national leaders and from the subsequent history of the nation that such influence was never intended to be prohibited. Separation of church and state and the influence of religion in government are two very different things. Obviously, the term "establishment of religion" had a special meaning in 1789 which it may not have in the mid-twentieth century. The term "establishment" is not used so frequently today in relation to church life. But whatever interpretation is given to the word, the Constitution cannot possibly be thought to exclude the influence of religion in national life.

It is precisely because religion was conceived to be of such great importance and of such fundamental significance that its distortion through institutions was proscribed and forbidden in the Constitution. Religion, insofar as it serves to point up man's essential dignity and his ultimate destiny, cannot but have great influence upon the total life of a nation. Adherents of the major faiths that have flowered in this nation are all agreed on the ultimate importance of man to his Creator. The life of society in general must be conditioned and determined by such a high regard for man.

The Christian in his devotion to God as we know him through Jesus Christ does not have to rely mainly upon legal devices or tax support for the promotion of his fundamental convictions. Any religion or any interpretation of a single faith should thus be free to proclaim itself in the open market place of religious ideas. Where legislation and favoritism have entered to protect a particular interpretation of a religion, faith has been distorted and the process of free search for wisdom has been stultified. When men have been able to rely upon governmental protection and special privilege, the process of earnest search and honest study of the truth of religion has ceased. For Christians, then, devotion to God as we know him in Jesus Christ will best be fostered by the constant necessity of proving and testing our faith in a free and uninhibited atmosphere.

America, having provided so great a measure of freedom for the exploration and expression of faith, ought to provide the finest flowering of men's faith. This, of course, we have yet to see. Nevertheless, of one thing we are very certain: special privilege to any single faith or interpretation thereof is not conducive to its fullest expression. It was this that the early leaders of our nation had the wisdom to discern and that Christians in our own generation have the responsibility to protect.

CIVIL RIGHTS

The most prized characteristic of American history is the concern for the fundamental rights of man. These were bought at a great price. We think of them as coming down through the Magna Carta, the Declaration of Independence, the Constitution, and particularly through the Bill of Rights contained in the Constitution's first ten amendments. The achievement and the defense of these rights have had a powerful influence upon the advance of our nation and upon all mankind.

But civil rights as we know them are not merely or primarily political concepts; their roots have religious origins. They will be maintained and strengthened only if men realize their spiritual nature. Correspondingly, one certain test of our spiritual depth is our concern for civil rights—for ourselves, of course, but even more for others.

Each succeeding generation becomes careless about the rights won for it by its forefathers. Only when some of those rights have been lost or seriously impaired do we awaken to their importance. Now for the third time in our history there has arisen in this country a realization that these rights are precious and that we might lose them. The other two times were, first, the period of the American Revolution and, second, the period following the Civil War. It is perhaps significant that the present wave of concern comes following another war.

Now, at a time when the world is being asked to choose between the philosophies of two great powers, America's most eloquent argument lies in its concern for the rights of people. Ultimately, the argument will be won on that ground. For, as the report of the President's Committee on

Civil Rights says, the United States is not so strong or the final triumph of the democratic ideal so inevitable that we can ignore what the world thinks of us or our record.[1]

SOME RECENT VIOLATIONS

A brief look at the record of abuses reveals the fact that, though the actual betrayers of our civil rights are few, these few have met less opposition than might be expected in a nation dedicated to those rights. Possibly at another time we or our successors will be ashamed of the record compiled during these years by local, state, and national officials as well as by private citizens.

These acts of betrayal may have been performed by those whom John Milton called an "Inquisitorious and tyrannical duncery." Milton Konvitz says of them: "Such men have always played a role in the American drama. To their contemporaries they have a Satanic character; they are seen as grand inquisitors and as men with an overweening ambition to win power sufficient to control the destinies of millions of human beings—push button tyrants. But to the next generation, or once they are defeated, they appear as pathetic dunces."[2]

For the record let us look at a very few of the cases in which civil rights have been threatened.

J. Robert Oppenheimer was, according to Dr. Vannevar Bush, "more than any other scientist that I know of—responsible for our having an atomic bomb on time." Like all great scientists he recognized that there is no monopoly on ideas. Out of a deep loyalty to his own country and a devotion to scientific truths he opposed some of his coworkers. His security clearance was taken away, and he was deprived of his position with the Atomic Energy Commission.

Probably no churchman in America has been more vig-

171

orous or impassioned than Bishop J. Bromley Oxnam in stating his conviction that the ultimate answer to communism is a full-rounded Christian witness. He challenged the now discredited methods of the House Committee on Un-American Affairs. He fought fearlessly for good causes even when they were unpopular. With the devices of publicity at their command, the House committee managed to attach guilt to Bishop Oxnam's name, despite the fact that he had disproved all their implied charges.[3]

A former president of Wellesley College and director of the WAVES in World War II with the rank of captain, Mrs. Douglas Horton, was asked if she would accept appointment as the United States representative to the Social Commission of the Economic and Social Council of the United Nations. She had been a strong supporter of Mr. Eisenhower even before his nomination as Republican candidate for the presidency. Mysteriously, the appointment did not come through. The only explanation offered was that senatorial hearings were likely to produce embarrassment to the President and his administration. Mrs. Horton had been an outspoken champion of intellectual freedom and other fundamental rights of Americans. Apparently the forces blocking her appointment were stronger at that time than the wishes of the President of the United States and the Secretary of State.

The most vigorous defender of civil rights in the United States is the American Civil Liberties Union. When its Indiana branch sought to use the War Memorial in Indianapolis for a meeting at which the speaker was to be Paul G. Hoffman, industrialist, former head of the Economic Cooperation Administration, and close personal friend of President Eisenhower, the request was denied. Even two such thoroughly tested champions of American ideals as the ACLU and Paul Hoffman were not granted the freedom to use a public building. The *Indianapolis*

Times editorial concerning the situation was entitled "How Silly Can You Get?"[4]

The intimidation of college campuses and the silencing of professors in institutions which should lead the way in American idealism is another of the casualties of this era. The wave of demands for oath-signing is but a symptom of the current distrust of freedom. Not all faculty members succumbed to the demands. At the University of California twenty-six professors who were dismissed for refusal to sign the oath were completely absolved of any communist taint.[5]

"The prize for this form of hypertimidity, however, should go to the Hollywood studio which, after six months of work, dropped its plan to produce a film based on the life of Hiawatha as told by Longfellow. Hiawatha had established peace among the warring nations. A studio spokesman explained that the film might be interpreted as a message for peace at a time when the communist peace drive was going on and, therefore, in the present temper of the country might be regarded as communist propaganda."[6]

People with a well-developed sense of decency are offended by obscene movies, plays, and books. The temptation is to eliminate through legal or police action what is deemed offensive to decency. But where to draw the line between indecency and "realism"? Is the gain in purity greater than the loss in freedom to exercise one's own standards? Is it worth the imposition of censorship? The film *The Miracle* recently raised these issues. A unanimous Supreme Court under the "due process" clause held that state agencies may not exercise prior censorship to determine whether or not movies and publications are "sacrilegious."[7] For conscientious people there is the everlasting problem of deleting genuine obscenity, on the one hand, and supporting the right of individuals to make their own selections in films, plays, books, etc., on the other. The "due process" clause in the First Amendment is one of the chief bulwarks in securing our civil rights.

The illustrations of impairment of civil rights are here drawn largely from situations created as a result of the international situation. This is perhaps understandable because the climate created by the East-West tensions has increased the number of civil-rights cases and highlighted them. The illustrations here by no means encompass all the civil-rights issues.

But all is not black. There are some highly encouraging signs. Walter Lippmann points out that there is a change taking place in the American scene. He attributes it partly to Senator McCarthy's overplaying his hand in attacking both Democrats and Republicans and partly to "the innate decency of the people." But, he says, the ultimate reason for the change is "the enormous emotional relief which has come since all the great powers have acknowledged publicly that there is no alternative to peace."[8]

HOW DID THIS COME ABOUT?

We are not primarily interested in the history of the impairment of our civil rights. We are more concerned about the means for restoring them. A brief look, however, at the ways by which they were impaired may give some clues for their restoration.

Communism has been charged with the blame for creating this chaotic and troublesome situation. It is quite likely, however, that the problem would have existed even if there had been no Soviet Union or world-wide communism. Rather, communism is itself the product of the same forces that created the present dilemma. The industrial revolution, which has affected every phase of modern life, has created the necessity for new forms of government, new patterns of international relationship, and new ways of life for almost everybody. Some people will insist upon holding desperately to what has been; others will insist upon life within the nation conforming to the new patterns that they feel are most desirable. The latter is what Russia has done. The Russians are obviously convinced that there is no solution to the present industrial revolution except in terms of regimentation and totalitarian dictatorship.

Deeply imbedded in the American way of life is a conviction that the rights of individuals precede the rights of states. Whatever pattern of state is evolved, it must accord with the elemental facts of human, individual rights. But at the same time individual rights must accord with the rights and well-being of other individuals; otherwise there would be anarchy. This, then, is our dilemma—how to preserve the fundamental rights of individuals and at the same time take account of the rights of all persons rather than of just a few. The unique genius of democracy seeks to secure and maintain justice for all. But justice for all requires concessions from individuals on behalf of the total society.

The problem of human freedom in our democracy and the issue of civil rights, which is so important a part of the problem, are thus an inevitable consequence of the world-shaking changes which have been going on around us. We have not traveled this way before. As Paul L. Lehmann says, freedom is in trouble not because of a conspiracy to destroy it "hatched by a small group of evil men" in a hotel room but because of the political, social, and cultural revolution that is happening all over the world.[9]

WHAT ARE WE DOING ABOUT IT?

When the progressively "reactionary" destruction of civil rights became apparent to those of us who had been taking them for granted, the tide turned, slowly but with increasing force. The first major blow in the battle to reassert the best in our American tradition of civil rights came with the report of the President's Committee on Civil Rights, *To Secure These Rights*, referred to above. This report was the result of an executive order of President Truman and is the product of a distinguished committee of citizens. It is a comprehensive survey of the status of civil rights in the United States at the time of the report. Though much grief and tragedy has marked the violation of civil rights between the date of the publication of that report and the present, it is, nevertheless, highly encouraging and heartening to note the gains that have taken place since 1947.

Another monumental work is the "Cornell Studies in Civil Liberty," published with assistance from the Fund for the Republic and under the general editorship of Robert E. Cushman. This series includes some half-dozen major volumes analyzing various phases of civil rights in America. They include a study of California's notorious "Tenney Committee" and a study of the House Committee on Un-American Activities. The list of excellent books appearing on this theme and dedicated to the furtherance of America's great tradition is long and impressive. Special mention might be made of two—Elmer Davis' *But We Were Born Free*,[10] and *The Fifth Amendment Today* by Dean Erwin Griswold,[11] of the Harvard Law School. The first kindled the imagination and self-respect of Americans in relation to their own glorious traditions. The second, from one of America's foremost legal minds, restores our sense of perspective on one of the most abused and misunderstood instruments for the protection of man's rights and dignity.

It is also of great significance that the Fund for the Republic, established by the Ford Foundation, has devoted itself entirely to the support of "activity directed toward

176

the elimination of restrictions on freedom of thought, inquiry and expression in the United States and the development of policies and procedures best adapted to protect these rights in the face of persistent international tension."[12] As a result of funds allocated by the Fund for the Republic many individuals and organizations will be presenting studies, experiments, reports, and programs related to these purposes.

Not solely American in its application or authorship but closely akin to the American ideals expressed in the Declaration of Independence is the Universal Declaration of Human Rights prepared by the United Nations Commission on Human Rights and adopted by a vote of forty-eight nations (of which the United States was not one). Granted that the ideals expressed in the Declaration of Human Rights may fall far short of achievement even in the nations approving this declaration, nevertheless it provides a goal, a standard by which nations may be measured and by which individual nations may appraise the practices within their own borders.

CHRISTIANITY AND CIVIL RIGHTS

On the façade of the Harvard Law School and on the walls of the chambers of the Supreme Court of Rhode Island in Providence there appear the words: *Non sub Homine, sed sub Deo et Lege* ("not under man but under God and the law").[13] The interrelationship of religion and the law as the protector of men's rights is perhaps so taken for granted in Western life that its origins have been forgotten. In this time of crisis we are impelled to look at the sources and the authority for those ideas we rely upon and for which our ancestors made great sacrifice.

Egyptian and Babylonian codes contain assertions of the sanctity of man's domicile and petitions for the individual rights of peasants. Charles Breasted in his *Dawn of Con-*

science (1933) contends that the Mosaic law and subsequent Christian ethical ideas drew substantially from the earlier Egyptian and Babylonian ethical developments.

But it was in the Old Testament that the concept of the brotherhood of man—involving man's responsibility for his brother—was inseparably related to the idea of a single God. Significantly, Jesus constantly referred to this God as Father. Though men may be unequally endowed with talents, they are, nevertheless, equal in the sight of God. The implications of this message are emphasized by all the prophets. The Old Testament is a history of the growth of this idea from a sense of special privilege for individuals and a single nation to an awareness of God's concern for all mankind. In the very last book of the Old Testament, one only occasionally quoted or referred to, appear the words:

> Have we not all one father?
> Did not one God create us?
> Why then do we play one another false,
> By violating the covenant of our fathers? [Mal. 2:10].

Kathleen W. MacArthur suggests that if the Old Testament prophets had not taught the moral authority of God over all life, the sanctity of the rights of the children of God, and the higher allegiance to God which even the most powerful earthly rulers are bound to acknowledge, it is unlikely that the human race would ever have developed its keen sense of justice now found in the great documents of freedom.[14]

It can hardly be insisted that democracy is the product of Christianity, yet it is true that democracy and a fundamental concern for human rights have generally prevailed in lands where Christianity has found free expression. The idea of the community as a fellowship of men living together under God's sovereignty and with ultimate allegiance only to him constitutes a radical departure in the human scene and one acknowledged only in Christian lands. Back of this is the parable of the Good Samaritan making explicit the fact that all men are neighbors. Jesus' insistence that all children are of similar worth to their heavenly Father makes an injustice toward one of those children a rejection of one's relationship to his heavenly Father.

The Apostle Paul spelled out even more philosophically the idea of the wholeness of society. He likened it to the body, one part of which could not say that another was dispensable (I Cor. 12:17). Or again he admonished against individuals using special privileges to the injury of others. "But you must take care that this right of yours does not prove a hindrance to the overscrupulous" (I Cor. 8:9). Freedom is not a privilege to be abused; it is a responsibility to be assumed under God and to be exercised with full awareness that one's neighbor is also a child of God.

The extent to which English common law and, hence, American law is saturated with religious interpretations of the nature of man and his rights is, of course, impossible to fathom. The origins are lost in antiquity and use. It is apparent, however, that the two grew up together, each strengthening and informing the other. Throughout the New Testament runs the assumption that love must be the dominant force in human relations. It is the failure to live in a manner motivated by love that alienates man from God and makes him sinful. St. Augustine recognizes this distinction between the ideal and what actually prevailed in the life of the early church. To him, "the great divisions within human societies and between human societies are between a society which is moved by the love of power and a society which is moved by the power of love. Love, as Augustine conceived it, is the single-minded will of every man to seek not his own but his neighbor's good."[15]

Then, to take a long historical leap, the Declaration of Independence reflects the tide of growing concern for the rights of man independent of the controls established by the crown or any other authority. Expressions such as "the laws of nature and of nature's God," "life, liberty and the pursuit of happiness," "certain inalienable rights," and "all men are created equal" reflect the yearnings and defiance of that period.

The deism which marked the thought of Thomas Jefferson was expressed in the earliest documents of American history because this attitude was shared by so many others of the same period. The thought of the times was saturated with religious presuppositions, though it can scarcely be said that the relationship between government and religious faith had been clearly defined.

We may hold different notions concerning the relationship between faith and law or government at the present time, but the thoughtful religious person starts with the assumpion that all life, including government, is held in trust under God. Both in the formative stages of American national life and in the present, God's sovereignty is acknowledged.

Man is endowed with certain inalienable rights, but he is also endowed with a creative capacity. He may attempt to make the kind of society which provides opportunity for the fullest expression of humanity. On the other hand, he can mar and destroy the well-being of his neighbor and ultimately of himself in exercising this creative capacity. When he chooses the latter, he demonstrates his understanding of man's relationship to his Creator and at the same time the extent of his own spiritual depth.

WHAT CAN CHRISTIANS DO?

We have reiterated that our response to the violations and defense of civil rights constitutes one of the tests of religious sincerity and depth. Defense of our own rights is a natural matter. Defense of the rights of others is a spiritual matter, to paraphrase Nikolai Berdyaev's much-quoted insistence that concern for one's neighbor's bread was a spiritual matter. We have just passed through (or we hope we have passed through) a period of intimidation and fear. Using the communist scare as a vehicle for their own exaltation, many people from all levels of society effectively silenced people of good will. They brought us to the place where many were afraid to speak aloud of the rights guaranteed to them in their own Constitution. We had become fearful that any person speaking critically of his government might bring reprisal upon a defender who championed his right to speak. People of stature and depth of conviction who expressed themselves fearlessly frequently suffered political penalties, loss of passport privileges, etc. We disavowed Thomas Jefferson's affirmation of 1801, "If there be any among us who wish to destroy this Union or to change its republican form let them stand undisturbed as monuments of the safety with which error of opinion may be tolerated where reason is left free to combat it."

Recently, 150 years later, during another period in which human liberties and civil rights were impaired, another President of the United States gave voice to a similar conviction:

We know that when censorship goes beyond the observance of common decency or the protection of the nation's obvious interest, it quickly becomes for us a deadly danger. It means conformity by compulsion in educational institutions; it means a controlled instead of a free press; it means the loss of human freedom.

The honest men and women among these would-be censors and regulators, may merely forget that the price of their success would be the destruction of that way of life they want to

181

preserve. But the dishonest and the disloyal know exactly what they are attempting to do—perverting and undermining a free society while falsely swearing allegiance to it.[16]

But the issues dealt with and illustrated so briefly are not merely political matters. They unfortunately reflect a quality of spiritual understanding and conviction.

THE CHURCHES SPEAK

The General Council of the Presbyterian Church in the U.S.A. issued in November, 1953, "A Letter to Presbyterians." It stirred up a substantial furor in the Presbyterian communion. When the smoke has cleared, this communication and similar ones by other denominations will presumably be regarded as part of the prophetic literature of our era. The Presbyterian letter states that the church, while loyal to the country in which it is organized, derives its authority not from the nation but from Jesus Christ, its sole head. Its ultimate allegiance is to Christ and his kingdom. This allegiance is relevant in considering the demagogues of today who preach that truth, if it aids and comforts our enemies, must be suppressed and who make suspect the ideas underlying "love," "peace," "justice," and "mercy." Presbyterians urge that we recognize that many of today's revolutionary forces are in part the judgment of God upon human selfishness and complacency. While this does not make the forces right, it does "compel us to consider how their driving power can be channeled into forms of creative thought and work."[17]

Speaking of congressional investigations, the National Council of Churches of Christ in the U.S.A. says that a basic threat to our liberty has been the "tendency on the part of our people and their representatives in government to suppose that it is within the competence of the state to determine what is and what is not American. The American way is to preserve freedom by encouraging diversity within the unity of the nation and by trusting truth to prevail over error in open discussion. The American way is to rely upon individuals to develop and express individual opinions. . . . Spiritual security can be achieved only by strengthening the nation's faith in God. The responsibility for deepening this faith rests with the churches."[18]

The demagogues and those who have sought to capitalize on the postwar hysteria for their own aggrandizement and gain have finally been resisted. The action of the Supreme Court in ordering the desegregation of our educational facilities (referred to in chapter v) represents still another major milestone in civil rights in America. The issue of civil rights, however, will never be fully resolved.

No day passes but what, in many communities of this nation, our hard-earned and sacred civil rights are endangered by the censoring of schoolbooks, the denial of employment because of race, the imposition of loyalty oaths upon public servants or upon churches, the denial of access to the ballot box, or some other means. Eternal vigilance *is* the price of liberty. We hold our liberty from God.

CHAPTER XI

CHRISTIAN VOCATION

The work we do and our motivations while doing it largely influence everything else in our lives. What man does, therefore, to earn his living cannot but affect all his waking hours. It is certain that our motives for earning our living and providing for the support of others reveal what we believe to be ultimately of greatest importance. This is the reason for the Bible's frequent references to man's work. It accounts for the long and inseparable relation between religion and work. For the way we work and the attitudes expressed in work are reliable evidences of our faith.

VOCATION

By an interesting process the work we do has, in many instances, come to be designated as our "vocation." The very use of the term implies something of our religious past. Vocation or "calling" implies, of course, a "caller." It is significant that this religious idea should have provided us with a term which is now, in the minds of many, completely devoid of any religious significance. One's vocation or calling, to most people, is simply one's job. But in the very process by which this religious term became almost wholly secular the nature of man's work ceased to be a religious function and came to be simply a means of earning a livelihood.

Once again, however, the word "vocation" or "calling" is coming to be used increasingly in its true sense. Every great ecumenical conference deals extensively with this word and its meaning. Scarcely a religious book appears without reference to it.

In 1952 there was held under the auspices of the National Council of Churches the first large-scale conference in this country on the theme "The Christian and His Daily

Work." Already in Europe there had sprung up in many different places centers devoted to the study of this problem by laymen from many different walks of life. Now the names of such places as Bad Boll, Bossey, Iona, Kirk und Werrld, Locum, and many others have become familiar to many in America. In this country meetings held in such places as Kirkridge and Parishfield are beginning to perform a service similar to that of the Laymen's Institutes in Europe. At least one major denomination, the Evangelical and Reformed church, has held national conferences for its entire communion around this theme. At the time of this writing other denominations, such as the Congregational-Christian and the Presbyterian, have, in the conferences of their national men's organizations, given major attention to this same theme. All these are evidences that there is a growing understanding of the Christian witness in work.

Many will insist that American life, both business and professional, is heavily influenced by "Christian principles." But "Christian principles" are something different from conduct or livelihood determined by a calling—by a response to God who is the creator and judge of the earth and all that is therein. Using Christian principles to temper the brutalities and crudities of an industrial society may actually be a form of easing the collective conscience and perhaps a self-righteous device for avoiding the more profound meaning included in the term "vocation." If, on the other hand, one means by "Christian principles" the determination to submit all ways and acts of life to God's judgment, one comes closer to the true meaning of the word "vocation" and to the most fundamental of all Christian principles.

Compelled as we are to reconsider our fundamental presuppositions, we are confronted with the fact that life either is or is not to be lived in recognition of God's sovereignty.

185

There is no half way. Trying to have it both ways produces split personalities and weakens both individuals and nations. As Christians we start with the assumption that all life is to be lived and all our work performed in devotion to God.

THE NATURE OF WORK

The term "work" for modern man means many things. It is that for which he is paid. It is what a particular industry contributes to society. It is the expenditure of energy toward ends that the worker considers necessary and desirable. It is the universal, age-long activity by which man seeks to sustain, to vindicate, and to realize what he seeks in life.[1]

In the process of work something distinctive happens to man. He is disciplined by the nature of his own work and the intent behind it. This expenditure of both physical and psychic energy shapes the thought and governs the heart of an individual. We have the common expression, "His heart is (or is not) in his work," meaning that he enters gladly into his task or does not. One of the factors determining whether a person's heart is in his task is whether he believes that the work is significant and that it fulfils his own inmost and deepest purposes. It is here that the biblical criterion serves as both a check and a stimulus. It asks whether the work being performed is actually in God's service.

But, just as the love of God is impossible without expression through one's neighbor, the work a person does becomes an expression of love toward his neighbor. Then, in the more inclusive sense, service to one's neighbor contributes to the benefit of community life in general. Thus the beneficial discipline to one's self, the service provided for one's neighbor, and the enrichment and benefit to the total life of the community are inevitable considerations in the Christian's evaluation of his work.

THE CHURCH AND WORK

In Judeo-Christian history religion and work have never been separated. Of course, there have always been persons and movements which have sought to isolate religion and make it something apart from common experience and everyday life. But also there have always been those who reminded their contemporaries that service to God that does not include the full expression of hand and mind is not service. The confusion in men's minds about the ways in which they might best serve God was, in part at least, responsible for the work system of the monastic orders. The phrase "to labor is to pray" underlies the monastic way of life. Ordinary commerce and family life seemed not to possess the quality that could identify it as sacred. Hence, only the specifically religious form of life under the auspices of a religious organization, the church, was thought to deserve so elevated a classification as "religious."

Recently a famed jazz artist renounced his mode of earning a living and entered one of the Roman Catholic serving orders. In explaining this unusual action he said, "I didn't find the completeness in jazz any more. I found that the religious life was what I wanted."[2]

No one may judge the motives of another, especially when he has little knowledge of another's circumstances. But in Protestantism the religious life in God's service can most fully be lived in the work-a-day world. It is here that devotion and dedication are sorely needed.

If faith and the full expression of religion are to be found primarily under the auspices of an institution, then it is not difficult to understand why the common things, the most ordinary experiences of life, were thought to be removed from religion in the Middle Ages. And then, of course, as the church was able to enforce the assumption that only activity under its immediate direction and responsibility was sacred, the institution of the church came to be identified as the only instrument of holiness and salvation. There is no doubt that monastic life contributed much toward the stabilizing of culture and mightily benefited all education and knowledge. Such gains, however, have to be weighed against what might have been the benefits of stressing also the Hebrew and early Christian convictions concerning the sacredness of work and the need for doing all work to the glory of God.

It was the church's monopoly on sanctity that ultimately ran afoul of man's discovery in the Scriptures that the whole of his life might be a form of sacrifice and dedication to his Creator. Men's relationship to God did not depend upon the mediation of a priestly class or an institution.

The Protestant Reformation emerged around this realization. It became apparent that there was no double standard in life. Either all life is devoted to God's service or none of it. No longer could persons who went into a monastery or who served primarily in the church be regarded as the only first-class Christians. The reformers sought to end "the monastic division between Christians who accept and Christians who reject this world."[3] The leaders of the Reformation recognized that responsibility lay, not in the nature of a person's act or the kind of work in which he was engaged but within himself. It was the person as the agent who finally determined whether a deed was sacred. Man's labor, thus, became his form of calling, providing "the outward condition for cultivation and proof of the internal wholeness of a regenerate nature and will."[4]

It was, thus, under the penetrating insight of Luther, Calvin, and other leaders of the Protestant Reformation that the term "vocation" came to possess its fuller and more comprehensive meaning. But the act of work or the

188

gaining of a livelihood in itself did not merit the designation. Man's labor had to become a means of serving his neighbor. The call which characterizes man's calling is determined by the way in which he serves his fellow man as a brother for whom Christ died. Thus, no matter what one does, if it is for the purpose of serving God and one's fellow men it merits the designation "calling" or "vocation."

The men and women who established some of the early colonies in America were imbued with the Reformation conviction that man served God only through the whole of his life experience. On this continent there have been numerous experiments designed to give witness to the totality of man's dedication. Some of these came out of what is known as the left wing of the Reformation. In some instances these experiments went so far as to prohibit private ownership of property and of the economic gains resulting from one's own industry and acumen, lest men be corrupted and forget that everything they produced was God's possession.

But in almost every instance a similar pattern ensued: diligence and devotion made for prosperity, and then prosperity dulled the disposition to grasp what was meant by dedicating one's work and possessions to God. The gains made both by individuals and by communal groups were taken as a sign that God had given his approval. A sense of righteousness and self-justification tended to take the edge off the ideal of service. Prosperity followed diligence; diligence was identified with righteousness. It was almost inevitable, then, that personal righteousness and the idea of vocation came to be synonymous. And from this it was only a step to the place where a man's calling came to mean "simply human work with God left out."[5]

There is an additional reason for the change in meaning of the word "vocation." Neither Luther nor Calvin nor any other creative mind of the Reformation could possibly have foreseen the wholly different society that was to come into being in a comparatively short time. The generation to which they gave their revolutionary ideas lived largely in a feudal, agricultural social order. But even in their time this order was collapsing, and the Reformation itself was made possible partly because of this collapse. The church, though all-powerful, offered no pattern under which men could adapt themselves to the changing conditions. Commerce was evolving fast and very soon would be accelerated even more by industry.

But the teaching of the reformers was also more readily adaptable to an agricultural era than to an industrial, commercial one. They were not aware of the potential power of economics, and were far more afraid of political than of economic tyranny.[6] The fundamental principle they taught, however, is as applicable to an industrial as to an agricultural society: all life belongs to God and man is but a steward of God's trust.

Working in a field with a hoe or a plow, knowing that the product of one's labors will provide bread for one's self and neighbor, is very different from working in an assembly line or an office where neither a man's tools nor the product of his labors are his own. It is not difficult, therefore, to understand why the original idea of calling or vocation has come to be identified with personal righteousness and integrity, whereas one's job or work is what one does to keep self and family alive. There is reason to protest against this evolution, however. Emil Brunner says that the idea of "calling" has been so disgraced and so denuded of its "daring and liberating religious meaning" that one might wonder if it shouldn't be renounced altogether. But in its scriptural sense the word is still "pregnant in meaning." It includes God's acts of grace and the concrete character of the divine command; to renounce it would be to lose "a central part of the Christian message. We must not throw it away, we must regain its original meaning."[7]

VOCATION AND AMERICAN LIFE

An American businessman, addressing the assembly of the World Council of Churches, reported that most of the businessmen and laborers with whom he was acquainted were not conscious of the call of God and Christianity in their daily jobs and professions. It is characteristic of today's businessmen to be more impressed by the futility than by the importance of their work. They work with anxiety and discontent rather than with happiness and a sense of fulfilment. "The gastric ulcer is the distinguishing badge of the man of responsibility today."[8]

Presumably the businessman who made this remark would be among the first to insist that the people to whom he refers are men of integrity in both their private and their commercial activities. They are, however, far from the Puritan pattern of living with its deep sense of gratitude for God's grace in Christ and of service to his community because all men composing it are children of God.

This is not principally a reflection upon the great numbers of us who are without such a motive in life. It is a reflection, however, upon the leadership of the church from which such understanding should come.

To probe into the reasons for this pronounced contrast between the ideal expressed in the Reformation and embodied in utopian experiments and the present relationship of the Christian faith to work would involve an analysis as broad and deep as the analysis of modern culture and the modern mind. But the Christian doctrine of vocation will be more adequately comprehended when this transition has been understood. A brief list of some of the reasons for this gulf between worship and our work-a-day lives includes the following: (1) People no longer worship with their work fellows. The old local community where men both worked and spent their leisure is no more. (2) Large areas of life once controlled by the clergy are no longer church-controlled. This wholesome separation seems to make workday activities non-religious. (3) An artificial hierarchy of work, with the intellectual at the top and the menial at the bottom, has belittled much useful and noble work. (4) Making work an idol, as if it were the only means to achievement, has given it false importance. (5) Work has been regarded by some as an instrument for evangelizing rather than a means of serving God through quality workmanship.[9]

In addition to these reasons for the separation of work and worship there is another so close to most of us that it is difficult to see it clearly. We have been taught to be proud of American industriousness. Our school textbooks emphasized the qualities of industry and frugality as a part of our patriotism and our religion. A freedom from the restrictions of rigid creed and orthodoxy in religion has freed the minds of modern men for exploration and intellectual activity. All these combine to make a vitality that we think is compounded of national enthusiasm and religion.

By implication, then, it has been assumed that America must surely merit this measure of superiority as a gift from God. Just as individuals came to assume that their good fortune must have been merited, so the nation is tempted. Thus have prosperity and religion been equated in the minds of many of us. But in the process the whole conception of Christian vocation has diminished or been largely forgotten. It is assumed that the nation's life can be transformed by its application to work. Salvation lies in industry, zeal, and perseverance. In a nation devoted to slogans, a very revealing one covered the billboards in the early days of the great depression: "Nothing can stop U.S."

192

But obviously something did. Two more wars thereafter postponed the necessity of having to face the problem as a nation, though many individuals had made a profound discovery. It is to that discovery that we now turn.

THE CHRISTIAN FAITH
AND OUR WORK

The wisdom of the Apostle Paul helps avoid the pitfalls of establishing a hierarchy of usefulness in work. He spiked a tendency to arrogance in the Corinthian church with the words: "There are many parts, but one body. The eye cannot say to the hand, 'I do not need you,' or the head to the feet, 'I do not need you'" (I Cor. 12:21). The inescapable fact is that we are members of one body. This is true for everyone, whether Christians or not. But it ought to be apparent to Christians. Of course, we do not become aware all at once that we are a part of a living community under God. A small child does not quickly grasp this fact; his experience is too limited. But for adults this fact crowds the airwaves and announces itself at every turn.

The Christian church must bear heavy responsibility for its own failure to confront mankind with this fundamental communal nature of life. In its own divisions it has often abetted those who would wilfully maintain a disunited society. But in still another way it has contributed to this difficulty. By specializing upon things "spiritual" it has given the impression that within the church there is a life that is different, superior, and distinctive.

The Evanston report says very bluntly: "The real battles of the faith today are being fought in factories, shops, offices and farms, in political parties and government agencies, in countless homes, in the press, radio and television, in the relationships of nations."[10] What could be of greater importance for the church, the institution dedicated to helping men find meaning to life, than making life meaningful at the place where men's interests are most fully engaged?

Rapidly becoming apparent in almost every major communion is the fact that the church is where its lay people are. The church is not the clergy, the building, or the liturgy; the church is the people—the people of God. But their worship is not "in temples built with hands"; their worship is the dedication of what they hold most dear and of what influences them most. This is their work. Thus, whatever that work may be, if it is needed, if it is a service to one's neighbor, if it is useful, it is one of the means of man's worship. This puts a very different slant upon the kind and quality of work one does. Inefficiency, slackness, or failure in craftsmanship through our own fault is as sinful as dishonesty, sexual immorality, or drunkenness. This is true no matter how little conscious craftsmanship is involved in the occupation and no matter what the social and economic system within which the work is done.[11]

There may be some of us involved in work that we cannot honestly reconcile with a genuine determination to serve God. What to do under these circumstances cannot be dictated by someone else. It is truly a matter of one's own conscience and his God. On the other hand, each year a mighty army of young people is faced with the decision of choosing a lifework. No longer is it necessary for them to assume that their Christian service and their dedication to God can be proved only or even primarily if they enter into professional churchwork. It should be apparent to us that the laymen who carry their dedication into their every day life are the church. This is not to say that leadership activities within the church are any less important—certainly not. Among other things, they help interpret man's relationship to God in all his work. Obviously, such tasks are of immense and strategic importance.

By now some surely will have said, "Yes, but you haven't

faced the real problem of present-day work and the obstacles it presents to Christian vocation. The real problem is that in an industrial society there are so many monotonous, uncreative jobs about which one can hardly feel any sense of vocation." This seems correct. Tacking on a gospel to the performance of these tasks may ease the burden of them for some people, but the overwhelming proportion of those involved in monotonous tasks will not find them sweetened by any undergirding by the Gospel. But what is true of the "meaningless," monotonous, and debilitating jobs is also true of the most highly creative jobs if both have to be done. The same questions must be asked of them as of any other work: Are they necessary? Do they contribute to human well-being? Any thoughtful person must recognize that the garbage collector makes a distinctive and utterly essential contribution to society.

Truly, "the layman is the bridge by which the church crosses over into the life of the work-a-day world. . . . The layman is the point where the church makes its main contact with the world. When a layman leaves his job for the day because of him it can be said, 'the church was there.' "[12]

Christian vocation, then, means the dedication of a person's self in that part of his life which occupies a large portion of his waking hours and which conditions almost everything else about him.

A very partial and limited understanding of God's service and of the Christian Gospel has brought us to this separation between what is sacred and what is secular in work. It is the outgrowth of a misunderstanding of the nature of the Gospel. For everything in the unfolding understanding of our faith denies this separation. The fuller awareness of God's claim upon our whole life makes our life very different from one divided between the sacred and the secular. Cameron P. Hall has stated this with rich comprehension:

The concept of Vocation—in office or store, in home or classroom, in factory or on the soil, must be based upon the *whole Gospel*. Certainly it cannot rest upon text or special references to daily work in scriptures. A sense of work as vocation must be rooted in the nature of God as seen in Christ. God is Creator but He is also Judge. God is not only Judge but He is also Redeemer. He is all of these in respect to the daily work which men do to live.[13]

We have said little in this discussion of Christian vocation about the ways by which we become more fully conscious of the spiritual significance of our work. The disciplines and study necessary for this achievement, just as for any other, deserve a chapter to themselves. The achievement is not accomplished by wishful thinking. We have here been primarily concerned with establishing the fact that the deeply meaningful understanding of Christian vocation sought throughout all ages but clarified anew in the Protestant Reformation again confronts our generation. Both the imminence of its claim upon us and the consequences of its rejection constitute a handwriting on the wall.

Here, then, in the renewed understanding of Christian vocation is solid ground for discovering the fuller meaning of life itself. In the final analysis, our faith and our spiritual maturity are tested by the manner in which we engage in our daily work.

NOTES

NOTES TO INTRODUCTION

1. Of course there is no single "American theology." There is, however, a kind of lowest common denominator of theological convictions held by a substantial portion of Americans past or present. These have influenced and are influencing our national life.

NOTES TO CHAPTER I

1. Quoted in Wade Crawford Barclay's *The Church and a Christian Society* (Cincinnati: Abingdon Press, 1939), pp. 47–48.

2. George F. Thomas, *Christian Ethics and Moral Philosophy* (New York: Charles Scribner's Sons, 1955), p. 215.

3. *The Children of Light and the Children of Darkness* (New York: Charles Scribner's Sons, 1944), p. xi.

4. Thomas, *op. cit.*, p. 256.

5. George A. Hillery, Jr., "Definitions of Community: Areas of Agreement," *Rural Sociology*, XX (June, 1955), 111.

6. "The Responsible Society," *Christianity and Crisis*, November 15, 1954.

7. *Ibid.*

8. Roger L. Shinn, "Evangelism, Stewardship and Social Action," *Social Action*, September, 1955.

NOTES TO CHAPTER II

1. See John Bennett's discussion of this issue in *Christian Values and Economic Life* ("Series on Ethics and Economics of Society" [New York: Harper & Bros., 1954]), p. 23.

2. Richard H. Tawney, *Religion and the Rise of Capitalism* (reprint; London: John Murray, 1943), p. 31.

3. J. H. Oldham, *The Oxford Conference: Official Report* (Chicago: Willett, Clark & Co., 1937), pp. 75–76.

4. *Man's Disorder and God's Design* ("Amsterdam Assembly Series" [New York: Harper & Bros., 1948]), III, 189–90.
5. *Evanston Speaks* (New York: World Council of Churches, 1954), pp. 26–27.
6. *The Responsibility of Christians in an Interdependent Economic World* ("Detroit Conference Statement and Reports" [New York: Department of the Church and Economic Life, Federal Council of Churches of Christ in America, 1950]), pp. 1–3.
7. *Christian Principles and Assumptions for Economic Life* (New York: Department of Church and Economic Life, National Council of the Churches of Christ in the United States of America [hereafter referred to as "National Council of Churches"], 1954).
8. *A Christian Economy* (New York: Macmillan Co., 1954), p. 139.

NOTES TO CHAPTER III
1. *American Capitalism* (Boston: Houghton Mifflin Co., 1952), p. 121.
2. *What the Union Can Do: Working with Churches* (Union Leadership Training Project Instructor's Manual) (Chicago: University of Chicago Industrial Relations Center, University College, 1949), p. 4.
3. Lloyd G. Reynolds, *Labor Economics and Labor Relations* (New York: Prentice-Hall, Inc., 1949), p. 446.
4. *The Church and Industrial Relations* (New York: Department of Social Education in Action, Board of Christian Education, Presbyterian Church, U.S.A.), p. 13.
5. *Causes of Industrial Peace under Collective Bargaining: Thirteen Case Studies* (Washington, D.C.: National Planning Association, 1953).
6. Frederick H. Harbison and John R. Coleman, "Working Harmony: A Summary of the Collective Bargaining Relationship in 18 Companies," Case Study No. 13 in *Causes of Industrial Peace under Collective Bargaining*, p. 57.

7. American Business Leaders, *Human Relations in Modern Business* (New York: Prentice-Hall, Inc., 1949), pp. 10, 11, 28.

8. *Union Membership as a Condition of Employment* (New York: Department of Church and Economic Life, National Council of Churches, 1956).

9. William Temple, *Christianity and the Social Order* (3d ed.; London: Student Christian Movement Press, 1950), p. 95.

10. Walter G. Muelder, "The Church and Labor Movement," *Religion in Life*, XVI (1947), 485.

11. *Labor Sunday Message, 1953* (New York: Department of Church and Economic Life, National Council of Churches).

12. *Ibid.*

NOTES TO CHAPTER IV

1. Leonard H. Schoff, *A National Agricultural Policy* (New York: Harper & Bros., 1950), pp. 59–60.

2. *Economic Policy for American Agriculture* (New York: Committee for Economic Development, 1956), p. 6.

3. Rainer Schickele, *Agricultural Policy* (New York: McGraw-Hill Book Co., 1954), p. 124.

4. D. Gale Johnson, "The Role of Farm Price in Agricultural Production," *United States Agriculture* (Harriman, N.Y.: American Assembly, Columbia University, 1955), p. 48.

5. *Full Prosperity for Agriculture* (Washington, D.C.: Conference on Economic Progress, 1955), p. 30.

6. Walter W. Wilcox, *Social Responsibility in Farm Leadership* (New York: Harper & Bros., 1956), p. 28.

7. Schickele, *op. cit.*, p. 163.

8. T. W. Schultz, *Production and Welfare of Agriculture* (New York: Macmillan Co., 1950), p. 150.

9. *Turning the Searchlight on Farm Policy* (Chicago: Farm Foundation, 1952), p. 68.

10. *Op. cit.*, p. 75.

11. Leonard H. Schoff, *A National Rural Policy for All the People of the United States* (New York: Teachers College, Columbia University, 1955), p. 16.

12. Walter R. Goldschmidt, *As You Sow* (New York: Harcourt, Brace & Co., 1947).

13. John D. Black and James T. Bonnen, *A Balanced United States Agriculture in 1965* (Special Report No. 42 [New York: Agriculture Committee, National Planning Association, 1956]), p. 26.

14. *Economic Policy for American Agriculture*, p. 27.

15. Schoff, *A National Rural Policy for All the People of the United States*, pp. 5, 6.

16. *The Christian Conscience and the Conservation of National Resources* (New York: National Council of Churches, 1956). The study conference was held in Pittsburgh, Pa., April 12–15, 1956.

17. See, for example, *Proceedings of the Conference on a Protestant Program for the Family Farm* (New York: Federal Council of Churches of Christ in America, 1949).

18. Benson Y. Landis (ed.), "The Social Ideals of the Churches for Agricultural and Rural Life: Pronouncements by Official Protestant Agencies," *Christian Rural Fellowship Bulletin*, No. 73 (June, 1942), p. 42.

19. "Report of a Conference on the Churches and Agricultural Policy," *Information Service*, September 1, 1951.

20. *Ibid.*, p. 3.

NOTES TO CHAPTER V

1. *An American Dilemma* (New York: Harper & Bros., 1944).

2. *Ibid.*, p. 61.

3. *Race—What Does the Bible Say?* (Roodepoort, Transvaal: Christian Council of South Africa, 1952); quoted from a digest prepared by the Council for Social Action, Congregational-Christian Churches (New York), 1956.

4. *A Message for Race Relations Sunday*, February 13, 1955 (New York: National Council of Churches).

5. *The Church amid Racial and Ethnic Tensions* ("Ecumenical Studies" [New York: World Council of Churches, 1954]), p. 7.

6. *The Christian Church and Race* ("Pamphlet Library on the Church and Minority Peoples" [New York: Federal Council of Churches of Christ in America, 1945]).

7. Yves M. J. Congar, *The Catholic Church and the Race Question* (Paris: UNESCO, 1953), p. 56.

8. *Southern Union News*, Summer, 1955.

9. Walter Sykes, *The Church and Social Responsibility* (Nashville: Abingdon-Cokesbury Press, 1953), p. 72.

10. Frank Loescher, *The Protestant Church and the Negro* (New York: Association Press, 1948).

11. Benjamin Mays, "I Am Glad I Could Report Progress," *Advance*, March 22, 1954.

12. Lee Nichols, *Breakthrough on the Color Front* (New York: Random House, 1954), p. 6.

13. Alan Paton, "The Negro in America Today," reprinted from *Collier's*, October 15 and 29, 1954.

14. Horace Cayton and George S. Mitchell, *Black Workers and the New Unions* (Chapel Hill, N.C.: University of North Carolina Press, 1939), p. 183.

15. Chester Bowles "The Negro—Progress and Challenge," *New York Times Magazine*, February 7, 1954.

16. *Op. cit.*, p. 19.

17. J. H. Oldham, *The Oxford Conference: Official Reports, Section on Church and Community* (Chicago: Willett, Clark & Co., 1937), p. 60.

18. *The Churches and Segregation* (New York: General Board, National Council of Churches, 1952), p. 5. An official statement and resolution.

19. S. Garry Oniki, "Interracial Churches in American Protestantism," *Social Action*, January 15, 1950.

20. *About Racially Inclusive Churches* (Interracial Bulletin No. 85 [New York: Department of Racial and Cultural Relations, National Council of Churches, n.d.]).

21. Yoshio Fukuyama, *Segregation and Inclusiveness of Protestant Churches in Metropolitan Chicago: A Progress Re-*

port (Chicago: Bureau of Research and Planning, Chicago Church Federation, 1955).

22. John H. Marion, "Parsons' Revolt," *Outlook*, February, 1956; quoted in *Information Service*, April 14, 1956.

23. Quoted in William Atwood, "A New Look at Americans," *Look*, July 12, 1955, p. 54.

24. Robert Redfield, "What Do We Know about Race?" *Scientific Monthly*, September, 1943, p. 200.

25. *Op. cit.*

26. "Intergroup Relations: Report of Section 5, Paragraph 19," in *Evanston Speaks: Reports from the Second Assembly of the World Council of Churches* (New York: World Council of Churches, 1954), p. 54.

NOTES TO CHAPTER VI

1. R. N. Carew Hunt, *Theory and Practice of Communism* (New York: Macmillan Co., 1951), p. 4.

2. Milton Mayer, *What Is Communism?* ("University of Chicago Round Table," No. 439), August 18, 1946.

3. Walter Crosby Eils, "Battle Ideas To Win World's Youth," *Think*, August, 1955.

4. *New York Times Magazine*, November 27, 1955.

5. *New York Times*, July 30, 1950.

6. *The Age of Confusion* ("University of Chicago Round Table," No. 769), December 21, 1952.

7. Creighton Lacy, "When Christians Support Marx," *Christian Century*, February 23, 1955.

8. Reinhold Niebuhr, "The False Defense of Christianity," *Christianity and Crisis*, June 12, 1950.

9. *Man's Disorder and God's Design* (New York: Harper & Bros., [1948]), III, 194.

10. Alexander Miller, *The Christian Significance of Karl Marx* (New York: Macmillan Co., 1947), p. 75.

11. Edward Heimann, "Comparative Economic Systems," in *Goals of Economic Life*, ed. A. Dudley Ward (New York: Harper & Bros., 1953), p. 141.

12. A. William Loos *et al., Two Giants and One World* (New York: Friendship Press, 1948), p. 30.

13. John C. Bennett, *Christianity and Communism* (Haddam House Book; New York: Association Press, 1948), pp. 46–47.

NOTES TO CHAPTER VII

1. F. Ernest Johnson, "Protestant Social Work," *Social Welfare Yearbook, 1954;* reprinted by Department of Social Welfare, National Council of Churches (New York, 1954), p. 1.

2. Shelby M. Harrison, *Religion and Social Work* (New York: Department of Christian Social Relations, Federal Council of Churches of Christ in America, 1950), p. 4.

3. Horace Cayton and Setsuko M. Nishi, *The Changing Scene (The Churches and Social Welfare,* Vol. II [New York: National Council of Churches, 1955]), p. 28.

4. *Ibid.,* p. 123.

5. *Ibid.,* p. 16.

6. E. Theodore Bachmann (ed.), *The Activating Concern (The Churches and Social Welfare,* Vol. I [New York: National Council of Churches, 1955]), p. 2.

7. Charles G. Chakarian, "Distinctive Contributions of Church-related Welfare Agencies and Institutions in *The Churches and Social Welfare,*" *Hartford Seminary Bulletin,* No. 20 (Fall, 1955), p. 34.

8. Arnold J. Toynbee, "Not the Age of Atoms but of Welfare for All," *New York Times Magazine,* October 21, 1951.

9. Cayton and Nishi, *op. cit.,* p. 156.

NOTES TO CHAPTER VIII

1. *Church and Community* (Christian Rural Fellowship Bulletin No. 78 [January, 1943]).

2. Quoted in Raymond B. Allen, "Professional Education in the Service of Health," *Annals of the American Academy of Political and Social Science,* January, 1951, p. 11.

3. William Alfred Sawyer, "Medical Care in Industry," *Annals of the American Academy of Political and Social Science*, January, 1951, p. 152.

4. Dean A. Clark and Cozette Hapney, "Group Practice," *Annals of the American Academy of Political and Social Science*, January, 1951, p. 49.

5. Howard A. Rusk and Eugene J. Taylor, "Rehabilitation," *Annals of the American Academy of Political and Social Science*, January, 1951, p. 139.

6. Harry Becker, "Organized Labor and the Problem of Medical Care," *Annals of the American Academy of Political and Social Science*, January, 1951, p. 125.

7. Clark and Hapney, *loc. cit.*, p. 47.

8. E. Montague Cobb, "Medical Care for Minority Groups," *Annals of the American Academy of Political and Social Science*, January, 1951, p. 170.

9. M. M. Davis and H. H. Smyth, "Providing Adequate Health Service to Negroes," *Journal of Negro Education* (1949 yearbook issue); reprinted as a pamphlet under same title by the Committee on Research in Medical Economics (New York, 1949).

10. Oscar R. Ewing, *The Nation's Health: A Report to The President by the Federal Security Agency* (Washington, D.C.: Government Printing Office, 1948).

11. C. E. A. Winslow, *Health Care for Americans* ("Public Affairs Pamphlets," No. 104 [New York, 1945]).

12. Raymond B. Allen, *loc. cit.*, p. 13.

NOTES TO CHAPTER IX

1. Leo Pfeffer, *Church, State and Freedom* (Boston: Beacon Press, 1949), p. 82.

2. A. P. Stokes, *Church and State in the United States* (New York: Harper & Bros., 1950), I, 165.

3. *Ibid.*, p. 546.

4. Pfeffer, *op. cit.*, p. 194.

5. *Ibid.*, p. 520.

6. Quoted in Stokes, *op. cit.*, I, 588.

7. *Church and State Newsletter*, No. 7 (September, 1951), p. 4.

8. Pfeffer, *op. cit.*, p. 178.

9. *Ibid.*, p. 474.

10. *Ibid.*, p. 348.

11. *Ibid.*, p. 373.

NOTES TO CHAPTER X

1. *To Secure These Rights* (Washington, D.C.: Government Printing Office, 1947), p. 148.

2. Milton R. Konvitz, *Bill of Rights Reader* (Ithaca, N.Y.: Cornell University Press, 1954), p. vii.

3. Bruce Catton, "Bishop Oxnam: Witness for Decency," *Nation*, August 1, 1953.

4. *America's Need: A New Birth of Freedom* ("34th Annual Report" [New York: American Civil Liberties Union, 1954]), p. 19.

5. Robert E. Cushman, "American Civil Liberties in the Mid-Twentieth Century," *Annals of the American Academy of Political and Social Science*, May, 1951, p. 5.

6. *Ibid.*, p. 6.

7. Robert E. Cushman, *Civil Liberties in the United States* (Ithaca, N.Y.: Cornell University Press, 1956), p. 13.

8. From syndicated column in *Chicago Sun-Times*, August 26, 1955.

9. *Your Freedom Is in Trouble* (New York: National Council YMCA/YWCA, 1954), p. 23.

10. Elmer Davis, *But We Were Born Free* (Garden City, N.Y.: Garden City Books, 1954).

11. Erwin Griswold, *The Fifth Amendment Today* (Cambridge, Mass.: Harvard University Press, 1955).

12. *Report of the Fund for the Republic, May 31, 1955* (New York: Fund for the Republic), p. 9; see also *Aims and Organization* ("Facts," No. 1 [New York, n.d.]).

13. Griswold, *op. cit.*, p. 33.

14. *The Bible and Human Rights* (New York: Woman's Press, 1949), p. 11.

15. Lehmann, *op. cit.*, p. 35.

16. Dwight D. Eisenhower, "Columbia Bicentennial Speech, May 31, 1954," quoted in *America's Need: A New Birth of Freedom* ("34th Annual Report" [New York: American Civil Liberties Union, 1954]), p. 9.

17. "Our Freedom under God: A Study Guide Based on a Letter to Presbyterians concerning the Present Situation in Our Country and the World," *Social Progress*, May, 1954.

18. Statement adopted by the General Board of the National Council of Churches, March 17, 1954, published in *Outlook*, April, 1954, p. 12.

NOTES TO CHAPTER XI

1. Paul Minear, "Work and Vocation in Scripture," in *Work and Vocation*, ed. John Oliver Nelson (New York: Harper & Bros., 1954), p. 35.

2. *Chicago Sun-Times*, February 29, 1956.

3. Robert Calhoun, *God and the Common Life* (New York: Charles Scribner's Sons, 1935), p. 48.

4. *Ibid.*, p. 44.

5. Robert L. Calhoun, "Work and Vocation in Christian History" in *Work and Vocation*, ed. John Oliver Nelson (New York: Harper & Bros., 1954), p. 84.

6. Alexander Miller, *Christian Faith and My Job* (New York: Association Press, 1946), p. 35.

7. *The Divine Imperative* (Philadelphia: Westminster Press), p. 205.

8. Irwin J. Miller, "Laymen Discover Their Vocation," *Christian Century*, September 15, 1954.

9. "The Laity: The Christian in His Vocation," in *Evanston Speaks* (New York: World Council of Churches, 1954), pp. 60–61.

10. *Ibid.*, p. 64.

11. W. G. Symonds, *Work and Vocation* (London: Student Christian Movement Press, 1946), p. 18.

12. *You, Your Church and Your Job* (New York: Department of Church and Economic Life, National Council of Churches of Christ in the U.S.A., 1955), p. 11.

13. *The Christian at His Daily Work* (New York: Department of Church and Economic Life, National Council of Churches of Christ in the U.S.A., 1951), p. 32.

SELECTED READINGS

CHAPTER I. CHRISTIAN FAITH AND
SOCIETY'S DIFFICULT PROBLEMS

BENNETT, JOHN C. *Christian Ethics and Social Policy.* New York: Charles Scribner's Sons, 1946.

BRUNNER, EMIL. *The Divine Imperative.* New York: Macmillan Co., 1937; Philadelphia: Westminster Press, 1947.

———. *Justice and the Social Order.* New York: Harper & Bros., 1945.

FERRÉ, NELS F. S. *Christianity and Society.* New York: Harper & Bros., 1950.

MATSON, T. B. *Christianity and World Issues.* New York: Macmillan Co., 1957.

NIEBUHR, H. RICHARD. *Christ and Culture.* New York: Harper & Bros., 1951.

NIEBUHR, REINHOLD. *The Children of Light and the Children of Darkness.* New York: Charles Scribner's Sons, 1944.

———. *Moral Man and Immoral Society.* New York: Charles Scribner's Sons, 1932.

PATIJN, DR. C. L. "The Responsible Society," *Christianity and Crisis,* November 15, 1954.

RAMSEY, PAUL. *Basic Christian Ethics.* New York: Charles Scribner's Sons, 1950.

RASMUSSEN, ALBERT T. *Christian Social Ethics.* Englewood Cliffs, N.J.: Prentice-Hall, Inc., 1956.

RAUSCHENBUSCH, WALTER. *A Gospel for the Social Awakening,* ed. B. E. Mays. New York: Association Press, 1950.

SHINN, ROGER L. "Evangelism, Stewardship and Social Action," *Social Action,* September, 1955.

THOMAS, GEORGE F. *Christian Ethics and Moral Philosophy.* New York: Charles Scribner's Sons, 1955.

WILLIAMS, DANIEL DAY. *God's Grace and Man's Hope.* New York: Harper & Bros., 1949.

CHAPTER II. ECONOMIC LIFE

BENNETT, JOHN, et al. *Christian Values and Economic Life.* ("Series on the Ethics and Economics of Society.") New York: Harper & Bros., 1954.

BOULDING, KENNETH E. *The Organizational Revolution.* ("Series on the Ethics and Economics of Society.") New York: Harper & Bros., 1953.

BOWEN, HOWARD R. *Social Responsibilities of the Businessman.* ("Series on the Ethics and Economics of Society.") New York: Harper & Bros., 1953.

CHILDS, MARQUIS W., and CATER, DOUGLASS. *Ethics in a Business Society.* New York: Harper & Bros., 1954; reprint, New American Library Mentor Book.

Evanston Speaks: Reports from the Second Assembly of the World Council of Churches. New York: World Council of Churches, 1954.

HOYT, ELIZABETH, et al. *American Income and Its Use.* ("Series on the Ethics and Economics of Society.") New York: Harper & Bros., 1954.

LINDSAY, A. D. *Christianity and Economics.* London: Macmillan & Co., Ltd., 1933.

Man's Disorder and God's Design, Vol. III. New York: Harper & Bros. [1948].

MUELDER, WALTER G. *Religion and Economic Responsibility.* New York: Charles Scribner's Sons, 1953.

OLDHAM, J. H. *The Oxford Conference: Official Report.* Chicago: Willett, Clark & Co., 1937.

PECK, W. G. *A Christian Economy.* New York: Macmillan Co., 1954.

The Responsibility of Christians in an Interdependent Economic World. ("Detroit Conference Statement and Reports.") New York: Department of Church & Economic Life, Federal Council of Churches of Christ in America (now National Council of Churches of Christ in the United States of America), 1950.

TAWNEY, RICHARD H. *Religion and the Rise of Capitalism.* Reprint; London: John Murray, 1943.

WARD, A. DUDLEY. *The American Economy.* ("Series on the Ethics and Economics of Society.") New York: Harper & Bros., 1955.

———. (ed.). *Goals of Economic Life.* ("Series on the Ethics and Economics of Society.") New York: Harper & Bros., 1953.

CHAPTER III. LABOR AND INDUSTRIAL RELATIONS

AMERICAN BUSINESS LEADERS. *Human Relations in Modern Business.* New York: Prentice-Hall, Inc., 1949.

BOULDING, KENNETH E. *The Organizational Revolution.* ("Series on the Ethics and Economics of Society.") New York: Harper & Bros., 1953.

Causes of Industrial Peace under Collective Bargaining: 13 Case Studies. Washington, D.C.: National Planning Assoc., 1953.

The Church and Industrial Relations. Philadelphia: Department of Social Education in Action, Board of Christian Education, Presbyterian Church in the U.S.A.

GALBRAITH, JOHN K. *American Capitalism.* Boston: Houghton Mifflin Co., 1952.

MAYO, ELTON. *Social Problems of an Industrial Civilization.* Boston: Graduate School of Business Administration, Harvard University, 1945.

MUELDER, WALTER G. "The Church and Labor Movement," *Religion in Life,* Vol. XVI (1947).

POPE, LISTON (ed.). *Labor's Relation to Church and Community.* New York: Institute for Religious and Social Studies; distributed by Harper & Bros., 1947.

———. "Religion and the Class Structure," *Annals of the American Academy of Political and Social Science,* March, 1948.

REYNOLDS, LLOYD G. *Labor Economics and Labor Relations.* New York: Prentice-Hall, Inc., 1949.

TEMPLE, WILLIAM. *Christianity and the Social Order.* 3d ed.; London: Student Christian Movement Press, 1950.

210

WATKINS, GORDON S. (ed.). "Labor in the American Economy," *Annals of the American Academy of Political and
Social Science*, March, 1951.

CHAPTER IV. AGRICULTURAL POLICY

BLACK, JOHN D., and BONNEN, JAMES T. *A Balanced United
States Agriculture in 1965*. (Special Report No. 42.) New
York: Agriculture Committee, National Planning Asso-
ciation, 1956.

CAULEY, TROY J. *Agriculture in an Industrial Economy*. New
York: Bookman Associates, 1956.

Economic Policy for American Agriculture. New York: Committee for Economic Development, 1956.

Full Prosperity for Agriculture. Washington, D.C.: Conference
on Economic Progress, 1955.

GOLDSCHMIDT, WALTER R. *As You Sow*. New York: Harcourt,
Brace & Co., 1947.

SCHICKELE, RAINER. *Agricultural Policy*. New York: McGraw-
Hill Book Co., 1954.

SCHOFF, LEONARD H. *A National Rural Policy for All the
People of the United States*. New York: Teachers College,
Columbia University, 1955.

SCHULTZ, T. W. *Production and Welfare of Agriculture*. New
York: Macmillan Co., 1950.

Turning the Searchlight on Farm Policy. Chicago: Farm Foundation, 1952.

United States Agriculture: Perspectives and Prospects. New
York: American Assembly of Graduate School of Business, Columbia University, 1955.

WILCOX, WALTER W. *Social Responsibility in Farm Leadership*. New York: Harper & Bros., 1956.

CHAPTER V. RACE

CONGAR, YVES M. J. *The Catholic Church and the Race Question*. Paris: UNESCO, 1953.

HILL, HERBERT, and GREENBERY, JACK. *Citizen's Guide to
De-segregation*. Boston: Beacon Press, 1955.

211

LOESCHER, FRANK. *The Protestant Church and the Negro.* New York: Association Press, 1948.

MABLEY, JACK. *Who's on First?* (Public Affairs Pamphlet No. 233.) New York, 1954.

MYRDAL, GUNNAR. *An American Dilemma.* New York: Harper & Bros., 1944.

Race—What Does the Bible Say? Roodepoort, Transvaal: Christian Council of South Africa, 1952. A digest prepared and distributed in 1956 by the Council for Social Action, Congregational-Christian Churches, New York.

REID, IRA DEA. (ed.). "Racial Desegregation and Integration," *Annals of the American Academy of Political and Social Science*, March, 1956.

SOPER, EDMUND D. *Racism: A World Issue.* New York: Abingdon-Cokesbury Press, 1947.

SYKES, WALTER. *The Church and Social Responsiblity*, chap. v. New York: Abingdon-Cokesbury Press, 1953.

VISSER T'HOOFT, W. A. *The Ecumenical Movement and the Racial Problem.* Paris: UNESCO, 1954.

WEAVER, GALEN R. "Racial Integration in the Churches," *Social Action*, December, 1955.

CHAPTER VI. COMMUNISM

ALMOND, GABRIEL A., et al. *The Appeals of Communism.* Princeton, N.J.: Princeton University Press, 1954.

BENNETT, JOHN C. *Christianity and Communism.* (Haddam House Book.) New York: Association Press, 1948.

HEIMANN, EDWARD. "Comparative Economic Systems," in *Goals of Economic Life*, ed. A. Dudley Ward. New York: Harper & Bros., 1953.

HORDERN, WILLIAM. *Christianity, Communism and History.* New York: Abingdon Press, 1954.

HUNT, R. N. CAREW. *Theory and Practice of Communism.* New York: Macmillan Co., 1951.

Loos, A. William, *et al. Two Giants and One World.* New York: Friendship Press, 1948.

Mackay, John A. *Presbyterian Statement on Communism and Related Issues.* Philadelphia: General Council of the Presbyterian Church in the U.S.A., 1953.

Miller, Alexander. *The Christian Significance of Karl Marx.* New York: Macmillan Co., 1947.

Oldham, J. H. *A Responsible Society,* Vol. III of *Man's Disorder and God's Design.* ("Amsterdam Assembly Series.") New York: Harper & Bros., 1948.

Reissig, Herman F. *Russia and Communism: Some Aspects of a Christian Approach.* New York: Council for Social Action, Congregational-Christian Churches, 1950.

CHAPTER VII. PUBLIC AND PRIVATE WELFARE

Bachmann, E. Theodore (ed.). *The Activating Concern.* (*Churches and Social Welfare,* Vol. I.) New York: National Council of Churches of Christ in the U.S.A., 1955.

Cayton, Horace, and Nishi, Setsuko M. *The Changing Scene* (*Churches and Social Welfare,* Vol. II.) New York: National Council of Churches of Christ in the U.S.A., 1955.

Chakarian, Charles G. (ed.). *The Churches and Social Welfare.* ("Hartford Seminary Foundation Bulletin," No. 20.) Hartford, Conn., 1955.

The Churches and Social Welfare. New York: Council for Social Action, Congregational-Christian Churches, 1957.

Harrison, Shelby M. *Religion and Social Work.* New York: Department of Christian Social Relations, Federal Council of Churches of Christ in America, 1950.

Johnson, F. Ernest (ed.). *Institute for Religion and Social Studies.* New York: Harper & Bros., 1956.

———. "Protestant Social Work," *Social Welfare Yearbook, 1954.* Reprinted by Department of Social Welfare of the National Council of Churches of Christ in the U.S.A., New York, 1954.

CHAPTER VIII. HEALTH

ANDERSON, DEWEY. *Health Service Is a Basic Right of All the People.* Washington, D.C.: Public Affairs Institute, 1956.

DAVIS, M. M., and SMYTH, H. H. "Providing Adequate Health Service to Negroes," *Journal of Negro Education* (1949 yearbook issue). Reprinted as a pamphlet under same title by the Committee on Research in Medical Economics, New York, 1949.

DYSINGER, ROBERT H. (ed.). "Mental Health in the United States," *Annals of the American Academy of Political and Social Science,* March, 1953.

EWING, OSCAR R. *The Nation's Health: A Report to the President by the Federal Security Agency.* Washington, D.C.: Government Printing Office, 1948.

GOLDMAN, FRANZ, and LEAVELL, HUGH R. (eds.). "Medical Care for Americans," *Annals of the American Academy of Political and Social Science,* January, 1951.

Health Care for Americans. (Public Affairs Pamphlet No. 104.) Washington, D.C., 1945.

PRESIDENT'S COMMISSION ON THE HEALTH NEEDS OF THE NATION. *Building America's Health.* Washington, D.C., 1951.

CHAPTER IX. CHURCH AND STATE

CUNINGGIM, MERRIMON. *Freedom's Holy Light.* New York: Harper & Bros., 1955.

DAWSON, JOSEPH M. *America's Way in Church, State and Society.* New York: Macmillan Co., 1953.

NELSON, CLAUD D. *Church and State.* New York: National Council of Churches of Christ in the U.S.A., 1953.

NICHOLS, JAMES H. *Democracy and the Churches.* Philadelphia: Westminster Press, 1951.

PFEFFER, LEO. *Church, State and Freedom.* Boston: Beacon Press, 1949.

STOKES, A. P. *Church and State in the United States.* 3 vols. New York: Harper & Bros., 1950.

CHAPTER X. CIVIL RIGHTS

CARR, ROBERT K. (ed.). "Civil Rights in America," *Annals of the American Academy of Political and Social Science,* May, 1951.

CUSHMAN, ROBERT E. *Civil Liberties in the United States.* Ithaca, N.Y.: Cornell University Press, 1956.

DAVIS, ELMER. *But We Were Born Free.* Garden City, N.Y.: Garden City Books, 1954.

GRISWOLD, ERWIN. *The Fifth Amendment Today.* Cambridge: Harvard University Press, 1955.

KONVITZ, MILTON R. *Bill of Rights Reader.* Ithaca, N.Y.: Cornell University Press, 1954.

LEHMANN, PAUL L. *Your Freedom Is in Trouble.* New York: National Council YMCA/YWCA, 1954.

MacARTHUR, KATHLEEN W. *The Bible and Human Rights.* New York: Woman's Press, 1949.

"Our Freedom under God: A Study Guide Based on a Letter to Presbyterians concerning the Present Situation in Our Country and the World," *Social Progress,* May, 1954.

To Secure These Rights. Washington, D.C.: Government Printing Office, 1947.

CHAPTER XI. CHRISTIAN VOCATION

CALHOUN, ROBERT L. *God and the Day's Work.* New York: Association Press, 1943.

HALL, CAMERON P. *The Christian at His Daily Work.* New York: Department of Church and Economic Life, National Council of Churches of Christ in the U.S.A., 1951.

HALL, CAMERON P., and GREENWOOD, ELMA. *You, Your Church and Your Job.* New York: Department of Church and Economic Life, National Council of Churches of Christ in the U.S.A., 1955.

MILLER, ALEXANDER. *Christian Faith and My Job.* New York: Association Press, 1946.

NELSON, JOHN OLIVER (ed.). *Work and Vocation.* New York: Harper & Bros., 1954.

SYMONDS, W. G. *Work and Vocation.* London: Student Christian Movement Press, 1946.

Abundance, economy of, 37, 45
Adler, Cyrus, 166
Agape, 18
Aged, the, 127
Agricultural policy, 69
American Civil Liberties Union, 172
American Federation of Labor, 49
American Medical Association, 139
Amsterdam conference, 24–25, 32, 43, 116
Anderson, Marian, 96
Atom, 41
Augustine, 178

Barnard, Chester, 30
Bennett, John C., 9, 119
Berdyaev, Nikolai, 181
Bible and rural life, 71
Black, Hugo, 165
Blue Cross, 140, 143
Blue Shield, 140, 143
Bowles, Chester, 112, 113
Breasted, Charles, 177
Brunner, Emil, 190
Bush, Vannevar, 171
Buttrick, George A., 166

Calvin, John, 39, 154
Cantwell, Newton, 160
Cayton, Horace, and Nishi, Setsuko, 126
Chicago, 95
Christ, definition of, 13
Christian principles, 185
Christian requirement, 26
Church, 21–23; and race, 99 ff.
Church and Social Work Conference, 130
Clark, Mark, 167
Collective bargaining, 62–63
Communism, 47, 108, 111; accomplishments of, 110; Christian critique of, 114–20; versus "Christian" economy, 47; claims of, 109; as religion, 107

Community, 23–24, 135–36
Congregational church, 155
Congress of Industrial Organization, 49, 59
Conscientious objectors, 159
Constantine, 152
"Cornell Studies in Civil Liberty," 176
Countervailing power, 51
Cromwell, Oliver, 154
Cushman, Robert E., 176

Davis, Elmer, 176
Day of Judgment, 4
Decisions, some major, 32 ff.
Declaration of Independence, 180
Democracy, 20; and Christianity, 178
Department of Church and Economic Life (National Council of Churches of Christ in the U.S.A.), 11, 31, 63
Detroit conference (National Council of Churches of Christ in the U.S.A.), 44, 45
Disraeli, Benjamin, 138

East-West controversy, 5, 31
Economic order, 45
Economics, 29
Economy, mixed, 34
Education, federal aid to, 162–63
Einstein, Albert, 10
Episcopal church, 155
Established church, 154–55
Evangelical and Reformed church, 185
Evanston conference, 25, 32, 43, 193
Everson case, 164

Faith, 2
Family farm, 79
Federal Council of Churches, 44
First Amendment, 149, 156–57
Fourteenth Amendment, 156
Fringe benefits, 60, 125
Fund for the Republic, 176–77

217